Keys to Understanding

by Jeffrey W. Hamilton

Keys to Understanding by Jeffrey W. Hamilton

ISBN: 978-0-6152-0064-4

Table of Contents

An Appeal for Reason

""Come now, and let us reason together," Says the LORD, "Though your sins are like scarlet, They shall be as white as snow; Though they are red like crimson, They shall be as wool" (Isaiah 1:18).

I find it amazing what is accepted as logic among the denominations. Some argue that God's Holy Word is too difficult for the average person to understand. Therefore, members are urged to let their leaders, who have gone to school for such things, tell them what God actually meant to say. Others argue that the Bible cannot be understood unless the Holy Spirit directly intervenes and grants a person the ability to understand the Bible. In either system the result is the same; when confronted with the truth found in God's Word they will say, "you don't understand!" They will happily ignore you because an "ignorant" or "spiritless" person cannot be expected to know about what they are talking.

Yet God has always invited reasoned discourse over His teachings. When God wanted people to understand that He alone is God, He invited men to bring their best arguments in support of their gods. *"Tell and bring forth your case; Yes, let them take counsel together. Who has declared this from ancient time? Who has told it from that time? Have not I, the LORD? And there is no other God besides Me, A just God and a Savior; There is none besides Me"* (Isaiah 45:21). God has no fear of man's

1

logic. *"For it is written: "I will destroy the wisdom of the wise, And bring to nothing the understanding of the prudent." Where is the wise? Where is the scribe? Where is the disputer of this age? Has not God made foolish the wisdom of this world?"* (I Corinthians 1:19-20). This is not to say that God will not reason with mankind, but to warn us that God is so far above us that He can make mincemeat of our best arguments. This is simply because all knowledge, understanding, and wisdom originates with God. *"For the LORD gives wisdom; From His mouth come knowledge and understanding"* (Proverbs 2:6). We cannot outperform God with what He provides. Hence, when God argued about the foolishness of idol worship, His case was flawless (Isaiah 44:9-20).

God chose the seemingly foolish method of preaching the gospel to save men's souls (I Corinthians 1:21). At its foundation, preaching is persuading people of the truth of the gospel by reason. *"Knowing, therefore, the terror of the Lord, we persuade men"* (II Corinthians 5:11). Hence, when we read of Paul entering a new city we find, *"Then Paul, as his custom was, went in to them, and for three Sabbaths reasoned with them from the Scriptures, explaining and demonstrating that the Christ had to suffer and rise again from the dead, and saying, "This Jesus whom I preach to you is the Christ""* (Acts 17:2-3). Paul's customary method was to enter a town and reason with the people from the Scriptures. When Paul moved on to Athens we read, *"Therefore he reasoned in the synagogue with the Jews and with the Gentile worshipers, and in the marketplace daily with those who happened to be there"* (Acts 17:17). Later Paul journeyed to Corinth were we once again find, *"And he reasoned in the synagogue every Sabbath, and persuaded both Jews and Greeks."* (Acts 18:4).

Paul was successful because he relied on God's logic and not the flawed methods that pass for reasoning among men. *"For though we walk in the flesh, we do not war according to the flesh. For the weapons of our warfare are not carnal but mighty in God for pulling down strongholds, casting down arguments and every high thing that exalts itself against the knowledge of God, bringing every thought into captivity to the obedience of Christ"* (II Corinthians 10:3-5).

God's way can be learned by men. God requires that all Christians learn it. *"Let no one deceive you with empty words, for because of these things the wrath of God comes upon the sons of disobedience. Therefore do not be partakers with them. For you were once darkness, but now you are light in the Lord. Walk as children of light (for the fruit of the Spirit is in all goodness, righteousness, and truth), finding out what is acceptable to the Lord"* (Ephesians 5:6-10). The Greek word, *dokimazo*, which here is translated "finding out" means to try, scrutinize, prove, test, or examine. Therefore, God is commanding each Christian to examine and prove what is acceptable to God. In another book, Paul said, *"Test all things; hold fast what is good. Abstain from every form of evil"* (I Thessalonians 5:21-22). Such commands require Christians to think, to reason, and to make judgments. The standard for all judgments is God's revealed word.

The need for learning to reason is evident. Paul warned in Ephesians 5:6 that there are people who will deceive Christians with empty words. Like a sugar laden desert, the words sound good, but there is no nutritious substance for the soul in them. Only by correct reasoning can we detect the good from the bad. To gain that ability, we must learn until we reach the maturity level of Christ Himself (Ephesians 4:11-13). So, *"that we should no longer be children, tossed to and fro and carried about with every wind of doctrine, by the trickery of men, in the cunning craftiness of deceitful plotting, but, speaking the truth in love, may grow up in all things into Him who is the head--Christ"* (Ephesians 4:14-15).

As we study together, it is my desire to show you how to correctly reason and how to detect and defeat the faulty reasoning of false teachers.

"For this reason we also, since the day we heard it, do not cease to pray for you, and to ask that you may be filled with the knowledge of His will in all wisdom and spiritual understanding" (Colossians 1:9).

Questions
1) Isn't appealing to reason canceling faith?
2) Some teach that man is too corrupt to be persuaded by mere words unless God directly intervenes. How would you answer this?

Knowledge: The Furnishings

"Woe to you lawyers! For you have taken away the key of knowledge. You did not enter in yourselves, and those who were entering in you hindered." (Luke 11:52)

In Proverbs 24:3-4 three main ideas are compared to a house. Wisdom is the construction of a house; understanding is the foundation; and, knowledge is furnishings in the finished house. Knowledge is the comprehension of facts. It fills our minds with pleasant and useful things.

In childhood we begin the process of learning facts. We go to school to learn our numbers, letters, and history. Often times we wondered why it was necessary to learn that Columbus sailed in 1492 or that "$a + b = b + a$", but as we age those seemingly useless facts become useful in certain situations. Just as a builder must have material on hand before he can construct a home, we need facts before we apply wisdom to our lives.

Moral instruction must begin with knowledge of basic facts. Children begin life with no knowledge of good or evil (Deuteronomy 1:39). As with Adam and Eve, we start life innocent.

God is the source of our knowledge (I Samuel 2:3; Psalm 94:10). He teaches us knowledge through the word he has given us. When we respect God, we take on the proper attitude to learn. *"The fear of the LORD is the beginning of knowledge"* (Proverbs 1:7).

The books of Proverbs was written to teach its readers. *"The proverbs of Solomon the son of David, king of Israel: To know wisdom and instruction, to perceive the words of understanding, to receive the instruction of wisdom, justice, judgment, and equity; to give prudence to the simple, to the young man knowledge and discretion – a wise man will hear and increase learning, and a man of understanding will attain wise counsel, to understand a proverb and an enigma, the words of the wise and their riddles."* (Proverbs 1:1-6). God doesn't want ignorant followers.

Rejecting Knowledge

Some people hate knowledge. They don't want to be bother with facts. We call these people "fools." *"How long, you simple ones, will you love simplicity? For scorners delight in their scorning, and fools hate knowledge"* (Proverbs 1:22). They do not want to learn (Proverbs 1:7).

Knowledge must be learned before you need it. If we put it off, it will not be available when our lives depend on it. *"Because I have called and you refused, I have stretched out my hand and no one regarded, because you disdained all my counsel, and would have none of my rebuke, I also will laugh at your calamity; I will mock when your terror comes, when your terror comes like a storm, and your destruction comes like a whirlwind, when distress and anguish come upon you. Then they will call on me, but I will not answer; they will seek me diligently,* but they will not find me. Because they hated knowledge and did not choose the fear of the LORD, they would have none of my counsel and despised my every rebuke. Therefore they shall eat the fruit of their own way, and be filled to the full with their own fancies" (Proverbs 1:24-31). Solomon warns of the regret of those caught in the trap of prostitution, "You mourn at last, when your flesh and your body are consumed, and say: 'How I have hated instruction, and my heart despised correction! I have not obeyed the voice of my teachers, nor inclined my ear to those who instructed me! I was on the verge of total ruin, in the midst of the assembly and congregation'" (Proverbs 5:11-14).

We have all met people who go through the motion of learning, but nothing manages to stick in their minds. Such people are prime meat for false teachers. "For of this sort are those who creep into households and make captives of gullible women loaded down with sins, led away by various lusts, always learning and never able to come to the knowledge of the truth" (II Timothy 3:6-7). A person who doesn't remember the truth will easily accept falsehood. A person who can't remember yesterday's discussion will not catch tomorrow's inconsistency.

The Israelites were told the good they should do, "but they refused to heed, shrugged their shoulders, and stopped their ears so that they could not hear. Yes, they made their hearts like flint, refusing to hear the law and the words which the LORD of hosts had sent by His Spirit through the former prophets. Thus great wrath came from *the LORD of hosts"*(Zechariah 7:11-12, see also II Chronicles 36:16). Many people are only willing to listen to things that satisfies their own desires (II Timothy 4:3-4). Because they do not have a love for truth, even when it hurts, they are easily deceived by error (II Thessalonians 2:10-12).

Knowledge isn't perfect

We must be careful not to think that knowledge is all that anyone ever needs. *"For in much wisdom is much grief, And he who increases knowledge increases sorrow"* (Ecclesiastes 1:18). It is a fact that each of us sins, but that knowledge doesn't solve the problem – it simply announces that the problem exists. The more we learn, the more we see the problems with which we are faced. However, the knowledge of a problem is not, in itself, a solution. Some problems cannot be fixed, and the number of problems in this world doesn't have an upper limit (Ecclesiastes 1:15). Concentrating on these facts can lead to a miserable existence. Why bother doing anything? It is enough to make a man retreat into a self-made shell.

The collection of facts can also lead a person into pride. *"We know that we all have knowledge. Knowledge puffs up, but love edifies"* (I Corinthians 8:1). It is so easy to slip into thinking we know everything there is to know – at least about the subjects we have studied. As Paul warns, *"And if anyone thinks that he knows anything, he knows nothing yet as he ought to know."* (I Corinthians

8:2). In other words, if you think you know it all, you haven't even begun to truly study the matter. Knowledge also doesn't bring sympathy toward those who have yet to learn. Too often we think that if we know something, then everyone should know the same thing. We must always keep in mind that people need opportunities to learn (I Peter 2:1-2).

The Bible warns us that we cannot know all there is to know. "*And further, my son, be admonished by these. Of making many books there is no end, and much study is wearisome to the flesh*" (Ecclesiastes 12:12). A person who tries to learn everything will simply wear himself out.

Learning Knowledge

Jesus gave the church the gift of teachers. "*And He Himself gave some to be apostles, some prophets, some evangelists, and some pastors and teachers, for the equipping of the saints for the work of ministry, for the edifying of the body of Christ, till we all come to the unity of the faith and of the knowledge of the Son of God, to a perfect man, to the measure of the stature of the fullness of Christ; that we should no longer be children, tossed to and fro and carried about with every wind of doctrine, by the trickery of men, in the cunning craftiness of deceitful plotting*" (Ephesians 4:11-14). Knowledge brings stability to the church.

While Jesus gave men in the church the duty to teach, they need students who will learn. A wise man knows there is ever more that he can learn (Proverbs 1:5). "*Give instruction to a wise man, and he will be still wiser; teach a just man, and he will increase in learning"* (Proverbs 9:9). What does justice or righteousness have to do with learning? You see, the wicked do not see any advantage in learning from God, so they reject his ways (Job 21:14-15). They may be willing to learn, but they have no desire to learn from God.

Learning will not take place unless there is respect for the teacher (Proverbs 1:7). Jesus's teachings were rejected because his audience did not desire to follow God (John 8:45-47). Paul told the Thessalonians, *"But we request of you, brethren, that you appreciate those who diligently labor among you, and have charge over you in the Lord and give you instruction, and that you esteem them very highly in love because of their work. Live in peace with one another."* (I Thessalonians 5:12-13).

Students must also have a love for the topic they are learning. Paul warned that some would be deceived and perish, *"because they did not receive the love of the truth, that they might be saved"* (II Thessalonians 2:10). That love for truth will carry us when the things we learn show us how wrong we have been. What learning would there be if all we learned was that we were right? To gain knowledge, we must be willing to accept the rebuke of the truth toward our shortcomings. *"Whoever loves instruction loves knowledge, but he who hates correction is stupid"* (Proverbs 12:1).

Learning is not a passive activity. Students cannot sit back as teachers shovel facts into empty skulls. *"Be diligent to present yourself approved to God, a worker* who does not need to be ashamed, rightly dividing the word of truth" (II Timothy 2:15). Both the student and the teacher should *"give attention to the public reading of Scripture, to exhortation and teaching. ... Take pains with these things; be absorbed in them, so that your progress will be evident to all"* (I Timothy 4:13,15).

The Gift of Knowledge

Among the charismatic denominations, the idea that a person must expend effort to gain knowledge is repugnant. Instead they will cite verses, such as I John 2:20-21, *"But you have an anointing from the Holy One, and you know all things. I have not written to you because you do not know the truth, but because you know it, and that no lie is of the truth."* In their minds, every Christian receives Holy Spirit and knowledge of all the truth. To say you need to learn is to say you aren't really a Christian.

What John is referring to here is a gift of knowledge from the Spirit of God, the same gift mentioned by Paul in I Corinthians 12:8. Paul's statements in I Corinthians 12 about the gifts of the Spirit is important because Paul points out that every Christian did not receive every gift of the Spirit. *"For to one is given the word of wisdom through the Spirit, to another the word of knowledge through the same Spirit, to another faith by the same Spirit, to another gifts of healings by the same Spirit, to another the working of miracles, to another prophecy, to another discerning of spirits, to another different kinds of tongues, to another the interpretation of tongues. But one and the same Spirit works all these things, distributing to each one individually as He wills"* (I Corinthians 12:8-11). It is a mistake to argue that every Christian receives every gift. In fact, some Christians received no gifts at all, yet the lack of a spiritual gift did not make these people any less a Christian.

Even for those who received the gift of knowledge, it was not a gift of complete knowledge. Paul said that their knowledge was partial (I Corinthians 13:9). He also argued that the gifts, including the gift of knowledge would be going away (I Corinthians 13:8-10). The ending of the gifts would come when the thing that is perfect arrives. Some try to apply this to Jesus, but I Corinthians 13:10 is written in the neuter – it refers to a thing and not a person. Also, he is not talking about something which becomes perfect, but something that is already perfect but has not yet arrived. James 1:25 calls Christ's law the perfect law of liberty. While Christ's law is perfect, it took a period of about 50 years for the apostles to record that law. Until that time, the gifts of the Spirit served as a partial substitute for the early Christians.

If you look at the context of John's letter, you will find that he was warning his brethren that false teachers (antichrists) were arising from among the ranks of Christians (I John 2:18-19). John is telling these Christians that they should be able to determine who is of the truth and who is not by the gift of knowledge the Spirit has given them (I John 2:20-21). *"These things I have written to you concerning those who try to deceive you. But the anointing which you have received from Him* abides in you, and you do not need that anyone teach you; but as the same anointing teaches you concerning all things, and is true, and is not a lie, and just as it has taught you, you will abide in Him" (I John 2:26-27). There should have been no need for John to write and remind them, but it appears they were neglecting to use the gifts God had given them. Much of John's letter contains criteria to use to determine who is of God and who is of Satan.

> We have books without number. More is being written, taught, and learned now than ever before in any age of the world; and yet all the education a man can get into his head could not save his soul, unless he knows and obeys the truths of the Bible. A man may be able to master half the languages of the world; hem may have read books till he is a walking encyclopedia; he may be acquainted with the stars of heaven, the birds of the air, the fish of the sea, the cedars of Lebanon; yea, he may be able to discourse upon the great secrets of earth, air, fire, and water, and still be lost for remaining ignorant of the Bible.
>
> Chemistry never silenced a guilty conscience, mathematics never healed a broken heart, philosophy cannot give hope in death, natural theology gives no hope of a resurrection. All these are good and useful for earth and time, but they never did and never can raise man above earth's level. So a man may be ignorant in those things, and yet, by the knowledge of that one Book – of one science – reach a home in heaven with God. We can get to heaven without money, health, learning, or friends, but not without the Bible.
>
> *Life of Knowles Shaw*, William Baxter, 1879, p. 128

While we do not have the special gift of knowledge from the Spirit, we do have the Spirit's gift of a recorded knowledge – our Bibles. By learning our Bibles we can know all things, just as the early Christians did directly. *"All Scripture is given by inspiration of God, and is profitable for doctrine, for reproof, for correction, for instruction in righteousness, that the man of God may be complete, thoroughly equipped for every good work"* (II Timothy 3:16-17). By studying the Scriptures we can apply the same tests John told Christians of his day to use to determine who is of God and who is against God.

Questions

1) Why is learning facts important?
2) Can knowledge save?
3) How can we avoid letting knowledge make us prideful?
4) What attitudes are needed to gain knowledge?

Understanding: The Foundation

"Therefore do not be unwise, but understand what the will of the Lord is" (Ephesians 5:17).

Sometimes when God speaks of "understanding," He means much more than a comprehension of facts. The Hebrew word refers to the intelligence of a person; his ability to connect ideas to gain further insight. We can see this in Job 32:11-12, *"Indeed I waited for your words, I listened to your reasonings, while you searched out what to say. I paid close attention to you; and surely not one of you convinced Job, or answered his words."* The word "reasonings" in this passage is the same that is translated "understanding" in other passages. Elihu stated that Job's friends were unable to use proper logic to convince Job of their belief.

The Hebrew word *biyn* and it various forms are usually translated "understand." It refers to insight gained by judgment as opposed to insight gained by experience. We often talk about the great wisdom of Solomon, but what Solomon asked God for was understanding. *"Therefore give to Your servant an understanding heart to judge Your people, that I may discern between good and evil. For who is able to judge this great people of Yours?"* (I Kings 3:9). This well illustrates what is meant by understanding. It is the ability to use reason to make judgment and come to greater insight. This is the word behind "understand" in Proverbs.[1]

The Greek word *suniemi* also contains the same deeper shade of meaning. It literally refers to the joining of two flows, such as two rivers coming together. It refers to the process of combining independent facts into a single comprehension of their relationships.[2]

Facts are useful, but God expects His people to combine those facts in reasonable ways to gain greater insight, much as Eli did when Samuel repeatedly awoke him at night. Eventually he understood that God was calling Samuel (I Samuel 3:8). The individual facts did not tell him this, it was his combining of the facts to reach a correct conclusion. Similarly, the disciples heard the words of Jesus, but they had no meaning to them until they combined the facts to understand that Jesus meant "doctrine" when he spoke about "leaven" (Matthew 16:6-

---

[1]Sometimes the Hebrew word *shama* is translated as "understand" though it is commonly translated "to hear." It means to listen with comprehension, much like our English word "understand." The Hebrew word *yada*, which means "to know," will also be translated as "understand." So every use of the word "understand" in the Old Testament does not necessarily contain this deeper meaning.

[2]Every use of the word "understand" in the New Testament does not come from the word *suniemi*. Some of the Greek words translated as "understand" have similar meanings to the English word. The word *neoe* literally means to see or perceive. The word *epistamai* means to comprehend. Sometimes words which mean to know or have knowledge, such as *ginosko* or *eido* are translated as "understand."

12). Understanding is the lighting of the bulb in our mind as confusing statements suddenly become clear because we see relationships between the facts (Matthew 17:9-13).

The Usefulness of Understanding

Paul told the Romans, "*I beseech you therefore, brethren, by the mercies of God, that you present your bodies a living sacrifice, holy, acceptable to God, which is your reasonable service. And do not be conformed to this world, but be transformed by the renewing of your mind, that you may prove what is that good and acceptable and perfect will of God*" (Romans 12:1-2). The Christian's religious service to God is reasonable or logical. We are expected to prove what is God's will for us. The same word for "reason" is used in I Peter 2:2, "*as newborn babes, desire the pure milk of the* <u>word</u>*, that you may grow thereby.*" God's word is reasonable and logical. When the Christian teaches others, he is expected to explain the reason behind his hope (I Peter 3:15).

This defense of the truth is done by the word of God. "*For though we walk in the flesh, we do not war according to the flesh. For the weapons of our warfare are not carnal but mighty in God for pulling down strongholds, casting down arguments and every high thing that exalts itself against the knowledge of God, bringing every thought into captivity to the obedience of Christ, and being ready to punish all disobedience when your obedience is fulfilled*" (II Corinthians 10:3-6). The "arguments" in this passage is sometimes translated as "imaginations" or "speculations." It refers to the worldly reasoning men employ against the knowledge of God. All logic is not good logic. There are plenty of people in this world willing to twist the truth to suit their own purpose (II Peter 3:16). The Bible teaches pure logic, unblemished by worldly desires. This is what Apollos had done, *"for he vigorously refuted the Jews publicly, showing from the Scriptures that Jesus is the Christ"* (Acts 18:28).

We must teach our children more than the facts of the Scriptures. They also need instruction in how to reason, how to construct logical arguments, and how to see the flaws in the reasonings of false teachers. Young children don't have the capacity to reason deeply, but beginning in the teenage years, young men and women gain the ability to reason. This is from where the claim of "rebelliousness" in teenagers comes. As the logic centers of their minds blossom, they question the logic behind commands. It often catches parents off-guard. They had become used to their children doing as they were told, perhaps with grumbling, but certainly not with demands that their commands be reasonable to the child.

Rather than be upset, parents should accept the challenge because this is also the age when children begin to think for themselves, realizing they are accountable for their own actions. Soon they will be considering whether to devote their lives to the Lord and they deserve reasonable answers as to reason for our hope. When the people of Israel returned to the land, Ezra gather people together. *"Then Ezra the priest brought the law before the assembly of men, women and all who could listen with <u>understanding</u>, on the first day of the seventh month. He read from it before the square* which was in front of the Water Gate from early morning until midday, in the presence of men and women, those who could *understand*; and all the people were attentive to the book of the law" (Nehemiah 8:2-3). Not everyone was gathered, only those who listen with a reasoning mind. "*Also Jeshua, Bani, Sherebiah, Jamin, Akkub, Shabbethai, Hodiah, Maaseiah, Kelita, Azariah, Jozabad, Hanan, Pelaiah, the Levites, explained the law to the people while the people remained in their place. They read from the book, from the law of God, translating to give the sense so that they understood the reading. Then Nehemiah, who was the governor, and Ezra the priest and scribe, and the Levites who taught the people said to all the people, "This day is holy to the LORD your God; do not mourn or weep." For all the people were weeping when they heard the words of the law. ... All the people went away to eat, to drink, to send portions and to celebrate a great festival, because they understood the words which had been made known to them*" (Nehemiah 8:7-9, 12). All the underlined words are the same Hebrew word, *biyn*. The act of teaching passes on the reason of the Bible to the student. Notice that they did not simply heard a reading or memorized a passage. The teachers went among the people to reason with them until they grasped the reasoning for themselves. This is why God's law affected them so deeply.

Understanding helps a person remember the knowledge he has gained. "*Give me understanding, that I may learn Your commandments*" (Psalm 119:73). It has long been known that men usually can only retain about seven facts in their short-term memory. However, if they can discover a relationship between the facts, they can suddenly retain far greater amounts. You can see this when attempting to memorize a passage. If you simply strive to memorize a series of words, the task is very difficult. You drop out odd words at the oddest places when you recite the passage. However, if you focus on understanding what the passage is trying to teach, the memorization goes smoothly. *"Make me understand the way of Your precepts; so shall I meditate on Your wondrous works."* (Psalm 119:27).

Understanding also aids our ability to learn new facts. *"Knowledge is easy to him who understands"* (Proverbs 14:6). Without understanding, you can hear things, but they never register and are quickly lost (Matthew 13:13-19). *"But he who received seed on the good ground is he who hears the word and understands it, who indeed bears fruit and produces: some a hundredfold, some sixty, some thirty."* (Matthew 13:23). As our understanding increases, it stimulates us to increase our knowledge. *"The heart of him who has understanding seeks knowledge"* (Proverbs 15:14; see also Proverbs 18:15).

We all make mistakes and must be corrected, but *"A rebuke goes deeper into one who has understanding than a hundred blows into a fool"* (Proverbs 17:10). A man of understanding is able to derive facts even from his mistakes (Proverbs 19:25).

Gaining Understanding

How does one gain understanding? Elihu told Job, *"there is a spirit in man, and the breath of the Almighty gives him understanding*" (Job 32:8). Herein is a major difference between man and the animals. Man is able to learn why things are the way they are. God is willing to teach this to us, if we are willing to listen. "*I will instruct you and teach you in the way you should go; I will guide you with My eye. Do not be like the horse or like the mule, which have no understanding, which must be harnessed with bit and bridle, else they will not come near you. Many sorrows shall be to the wicked; But he who trusts in the LORD, mercy shall surround him*" (Psalm 32:8-10). Try to explain to a donkey why he must take up the harness and plow so there will be wheat to eat in the fall — it just will not work and neither will the donkey. A man who will not understand is no better than an animal (Psalm 49:20).

A person cannot have understanding until he first has some knowledge. "*You asked, 'Who is this who hides counsel without knowledge?' Therefore I have uttered what I did not understand, Things too wonderful for me, which I did not know*" (Job 42:3) The knowledge of God's word gives us understanding. "*Through Your precepts I get understanding; Therefore I hate every false way*" (Psalm 119:104; see also Psalm 119:130, 169). This means there must be growth. Just as you cannot reason with a very small child, you cannot expect to reason about the Scriptures with someone who knows very little about them. "*Whom will he teach knowledge? And whom will he make to understand the message? Those just weaned from milk? Those just drawn from the breasts? For precept must be upon precept, precept upon precept, Line upon line, line upon line, Here a little, there a little"* (Isaiah 28:9-10). This is one of the reasons why the disciples appeared to be slow on grasping what was happening. They did not know enough facts to gain understanding as to why things were happening as they did (Luke 18:31-34). Then, in turn, the understanding that we gain makes it easier for us to retain additional knowledge. *"All the words of my mouth are with righteousness; Nothing crooked or perverse is in them. They are all plain to him who understands, And right to those who find knowledge"* (Proverbs 8:8-9).

Stubbornness prevents the gaining of understanding (Mark 6:52; 8:17-18). A person cannot be made to learn what he doesn't want to learn.

Understanding also comes by observation. *"The righteous see it and rejoice, and all iniquity stops its mouth. Whoever is wise will observe these things, and they will understand the lovingkindness of the LORD"* (Psalms 107:42-43).

But to really gain understanding, a person must apply what he learns from God to his life. *"I understand more than the ancients, because I keep Your precepts"* (Psalm 119:100).

The Limits to Understanding
"Who can understand his errors? Cleanse me from secret faults." (Psalm 19:12). It is very difficult to see your own incorrect reasoning. You reached your erroneous conclusions by a fault in your own reasoning, so until that fault is corrected, you will continue to make the same mistake. We need to have our path adjusted from a source outside of ourselves. *"A man's steps are of the*

LORD; How then can a man understand his own way?"
(Proverbs 20:24). When a person thinks he understands
everything, therein lies danger (Isaiah 5:21). No man
understands it all (Romans 3:11).

Understanding is not a guarantee of success. It makes
a person better prepared, but there are still random
events that bring harm to even the best of people
(Ecclesiastes 9:11).

The Gift of Understanding

Just as there was a gift of knowledge during the early
days of the church, the Spirit gave some the gift of
discerning spirits (I Corinthians 12:10).

Questions

1) What are the different definitions of the word
   "understanding" as used in the Scriptures?
2) What makes for good or bad logic?
3) How does a person learn to reason well?
4) Why is it that men can never have perfect
   understanding?

Wisdom: The Construction

"If any of you lacks wisdom, let him ask of God, who gives to all liberally and without reproach, and it will be given to him. But let him ask in faith, with no doubting, for he who doubts is like a wave of the sea driven and tossed by the wind. For let not that man suppose that he will receive anything from the Lord; he is a double-minded man, unstable in all his ways" (James 1:5-8).

Wisdom is a valuable commodity that few men appreciate. Job 28:12-28 is a discourse on how valuable and rare true godly wisdom is. The only reliable source of wisdom is God because God alone has the understanding of everything. Hence, for man to learn wisdom he must start with a reverence for God.

Wisdom doesn't just benefit the wise man. His wisdom becomes a blessing to those around him (I Kings 10:6-8). *"Who is wise and understanding among you? Let him show by good conduct that his works are done in the meekness of wisdom. But if you have bitter envy and self-seeking in your hearts, do not boast and lie against the truth. This wisdom does not descend from above, but is earthly, sensual, demonic. For where envy and self-seeking exist, confusion and every evil thing are there. But the wisdom that is from above is first pure, then peaceable, gentle, willing to yield, full of mercy and good fruits, without partiality and without hypocrisy"* (James 3:13-17).

All that Passes for Wisdom is not Wise

Frequently you read in the Scriptures the contrast between God's wisdom and the wisdom of this world (I Corinthians 1:20-21, 25; 2:6-8). Where godly wisdom benefits all, worldly wisdom seeks to benefit the individual, even at the expense of harming others. Worldly wisdom is selfish. "Wise" men of this world rarely accept the gospel of Christ because it doesn't originate with man. Accepting God's wisdom is admitting that their own ideas are less than God's (Matthew 11:25; I Corinthians 1:26-29). Worldly wisdom is filled with pride. *"Do you see a man wise in his own eyes? There is more hope for a fool than for him"* (Proverbs 21:2). A person who thinks he is already wise will not be able to learn wisdom. (See also Romans 12:16; Isaiah 5:21.)

Scholarship is not an indication of acquired wisdom. *"Let no one deceive himself. If anyone among you seems to be wise in this age, let him become a fool that he may become wise. For the wisdom of this world is foolishness with God. For it is written, "He catches the wise in their own craftiness"; and again, "The LORD knows the thoughts of the wise, that they are futile."'* (1 Corinthians 3:18-20). The number of letters after a man's name, even a doctorate in theology, will not tell you if a man is wise or not. Just because a man claims wisdom and others back him up does not necessarily make it so. *"How can you say, 'We are wise, And the law of the LORD is with us'? Look, the false pen of the scribe certainly works falsehood. The wise men are ashamed, They are dismayed and taken. Behold, they have rejected the word* of the LORD; So what wisdom do they have?" (Jeremiah 8:8-9).

Often times we mistake temporary success as an indication of wisdom. We consider wealthy men as having a good deal of wisdom. However, the Scriptures warn, *"The rich man is wise in his own eyes, but the poor who has understanding sees through him"* (Proverbs 28:11). Riches can come from successful dealings, but it can also come from deceit, fraud, and other unfair business practices. Riches can be quickly gained during times of ease and just as quickly disappears during difficult years. The amount of funds in a man's bank account is not a measure of his wisdom (Ecclesiastes 9:11). *"There was a little city with few men in it; and a great king came against it, besieged it, and built great snares around it. Now there was found in it a poor wise man, and he by his wisdom delivered the city. Yet no one remembered that same poor man. Then I said: 'Wisdom is better than strength. Nevertheless the poor man's wisdom is despised, And his words are not heard'"* (Ecclesiastes 9:14-16).

While age ought to bring wisdom, it is not always so. Elihu scolded Job's friends for this. *"I am young in years, and you are very old; Therefore I was afraid, And dared not declare my opinion to you. I said, 'Age should speak, And multitude of years should teach wisdom.' But there is a spirit in man, And the breath of the Almighty gives him understanding. Great men are not always wise, Nor do the aged always understand justice"* (Job 32:6-9). A young man who listens to and understands the wisdom of God can be far wiser than old men who do not heed the

God's teachings. We should not make the mistake of assuming that older people are always wiser. The world does contain old fools.

How Wisdom is Gained

Solomon asked God for knowledge, understanding, and wisdom (I Kings 3:9; II Chronicles 1:10-12) and it was granted to him. Solomon understood that one without the other two was not nearly as useful. Wisdom comes when things are understood – when the reasons are clearly displayed (Proverbs 14:8, 33). A wise person can then pass on his wisdom through teaching (I Kings 11:41; Job 33:31-33).

Generally a person accumulates wisdom over the years (Job 12:12). Experience teaches men what does and does not work. However, that experience must be coupled with God's teaching (Job 12:13). On our own, we will sometimes draw the wrong conclusion as to why something does or does not work. God keeps us in line with the truth through His word.

Like knowledge and understanding, wisdom only comes to a person who has a proper reverence for God (Proverbs 9:10). God is the source of all true wisdom, so to gain wisdom, we must approach Him for guidance. James tells us to ask God for wisdom and it will be granted to you (James 1:5-8). Our request must be made with confidence that God will grant what we desire. However, don't assume that wisdom is granted by God opening our skulls and dropping a scoop of wisdom inside. James does not directly state how God will give us wisdom; he only assures us that God is able and willing to do so. If you go back to verse 2 in James though, you will see that James is discussing the benefits of trials (difficulties). When we face and overcome trials, our character grows. He follows this section by encouraging his readers to ask God for wisdom. The implication is that God will give us wisdom by giving us plenty of experiences in life so that we can develop wisdom.

Some people claim to seek wisdom, but when it is presented they scoff at it and, so, they never find what they are seeking (Proverbs 14:6). Others are selective in what they want to hear. *"For the time will come when they will not endure sound doctrine, but according to their own desires, because they have itching ears, they will heap up for themselves teachers; and they will turn their ears away from the truth, and be turned aside to fables"* (II Timothy 4:3-4). Neither gain wisdom because they have rejected it.

True wisdom comes from righteousness and truth (Proverbs 8:6-8). This is because real wisdom benefits all people. Wickedness benefits no one. You can't learn leadership from the evil dictators of the world, nor can you learn wisdom from the morally corrupt. Godly wisdom cannot be learned apart from God. *"Although they knew God, they did not glorify Him as God, nor were thankful, but became futile in their thoughts, and their foolish hearts were darkened. Professing to be wise, they became fools"* (Romans 1:21-22). Only through God's commandments can we obtain wisdom (Psalm 119:98).

Therefore, it is God's law which teaches men godly wisdom (Deuteronomy 4:6). This law is referred to as God's wisdom (I Corinthians 2:6-8).

The Gift of Wisdom

God has given wisdom to many people in the past. The men who worked on the tabernacle were granted knowledge, understanding, wisdom, and skill in order to create the tabernacle according to God's pattern (Exodus 28:3; 31:3; 35:31). The leaders God chose were also granted wisdom from God so they could lead his people (Deuteronomy 34:9, I Kings 4:29-34; Ezra 7:25).

Some of the early disciples were given the word of wisdom by the same Spirit who gave others the word of knowledge (I Corinthians 12:8). These early Christians were able to teach wisdom and knowledge to their fellow Christians by the word given to them by the Spirit of God. The wisdom did not come from their own experience. The teaching was imparting the wisdom of God. Paul spoke of this gift, which we sometimes call "inspiration," in I Corinthians 2:6-7. *"We speak wisdom among those who are mature, yet not the wisdom of this age, nor of the rulers of this age, who are coming to nothing. But we speak the wisdom of God in a mystery, the hidden wisdom which God ordained before the ages for our glory."*

As the gift of knowledge, the gift of the word of wisdom passed way (I Corinthians 13:8-11). Yet we are not left without knowledge or wisdom. The Spirit had the word of knowledge and the word of wisdom recorded so that we who live in the distant years can still learn and benefit. *"... how that by revelation He made known to me the mystery (as I have briefly written already, by which, when you read, you may understand my knowledge in the mystery of Christ), which in other ages was not made known to the sons of men, as it has now been revealed by the Spirit to His holy apostles and prophets"* (Ephesians 3:3-5).

Questions

1) How can a person learn to be wise?
2) What are the different types of wisdom?
3) Are all forms of wisdom equally good? Why or why not?
4) Have the gifts of wisdom, knowledge, and understanding ceased? How would you prove this?

Suffering with Fools

No one wants to be thought of as a fool ...

(Wesley Chapel, Florida, 1995) Joseph Aaron, 20, was hit in the leg with pieces of the bullet he fired at the exhaust pipe of his car. When repairing the car, he needed to bore a hole in the pipe. When he couldn't find a drill, he tried to shoot a hole in it.

(Ontario, Canada, 1996) A man cleaning a bird feeder on his balcony of his condominium apartment in this Toronto suburb slipped and fell 23 stories to his death, police said Monday. Stefan Macko, 55, was standing on a wheeled chair Sunday when the accident occurred, said Inspector Arcy Honer of the Peel regional police. It appears the chair moved and he went over the balcony, Honer said. One of those freak accidents. No foul play is suspected.

We will go to great lengths to avoid doing foolish things
...
And still we manage to do so many things that are just plain dumb. If only we only thought about the situation more. If only we realized the more obvious consequences

---

of our actions. Perhaps if we learn why some people are foolish, it will prevent us from following after them.

A Fool Doesn't Want to Learn

"How long, you simple ones, will you love simplicity? For scorners delight in their scorning, And fools hate knowledge" (Proverbs 1:22). A fool doesn't want to take the time to learn, thinking that the knowledge he currently has is sufficient. Oh, he may act as if he is listening, but because his behavior doesn't change, we know he wasn't truly listening. *"But everyone who hears these sayings of Mine, and does not do them, will be like a foolish man who built his house on the sand: and the rain descended, the floods came, and the winds blew and beat on that house; and it fell. And great was its fall"* (Matthew 7:26-27). How could one be more foolish than to come to the Lord for His words and then give no thought for the future?

Oh, and you can't force a fool to learn. *"Though you grind a fool in a mortar with a pestle along with crushed grain, Yet his foolishness will not depart from him"* (Proverbs 27:22).

Inevitably the fool reveals his true nature. Foolishness is not something that is easily hidden. *"Every prudent man acts with knowledge, But a fool lays open his folly."* (Proverbs 13:16).

A Fool is More Interested in His Own Words

When a fool enters a discussion, he is not interested in learning. He just desires a opportunity to spout off what little he knows. *"A fool has no delight in understanding, but in expressing his own heart"* (Proverbs 18:2). And once the fool's mouth starts flapping, we are given full proof as to how little is there. *"A prudent man conceals knowledge, but the heart of fools proclaims foolishness"* (Proverbs 12:23). This is why wise men speak as little as possible (Proverbs 10:19). The more you say, the more likely you will make a mistake. But such does not concern the fool. *"The tongue of the wise uses knowledge rightly, but the mouth of fools pours forth foolishness"* (Proverbs 15:2).

Since a fool's conversation doesn't have much in the way of content, he makes up for the lack with a large amount of words. *"A fool's voice is known by his many words"* (Ecclesiastes 5:3). Watch the next time you see a politician interviewed. When the interviewer trips him up with question he wasn't expecting words will just pour out of his mouth as he frantically tries to think of a reasonable sounding answer. By the time he gets done babbling, you have forgotten what was the question. Meanwhile, it appears no harm has been done as he hasn't said anything of consequence anyway.

Fools are Led by Their Emotions

"The simple believes every word, but the prudent considers well his steps." (Proverbs 14:15). It is easier to

just accept what you are told. It takes effort to weigh the value of each word. Hence, a foolish person is easily led into sin (Proverbs 7:6-27). The wise person realizes that Satan and his followers lie (John 8:44).

Fools want to be right, but they don't have the ability to reason from the truth. Therefore, when they are caught in the wrong, their impulsive reaction is to fight. "*A fool's lips enter into contention, and his mouth calls for blows. A fool's mouth is his destruction, and his lips are the snare of his soul*" (Proverbs 18:6-7). He gets carried away by the emotional desire to win at any cost. "*It is honorable for a man to stop striving, since any fool can start a quarrel*" (Proverbs 20:3).

Nothing labels a man a fool better than a man's anger. "*Do not hasten in your spirit to be angry, for anger rests in the bosom of fools*" (Ecclesiastes 7:9). Yet a man's anger rarely solves problems (James 1:20). Righteous living requires consideration and thought. There are far too many traps laid for us by Satan. To give replies without careful consideration is unwise (Proverbs 18:13). A man caught up in the emotions of anger is not looking for the traps.

Not all fools blast out in their anger. Some hide their feelings and use subtle backstabbing to gain their revenge. "*Whoever hides hatred has lying lips, and whoever spreads slander is a fool*" (Proverbs 10:18). But it doesn't matter if a person's anger is dramatic or subtle, the anger of men rarely leads to righteousness.

Fools are Arrogant

"He who trusts in his own heart is a fool, But whoever walks wisely will be delivered" (Proverbs 28:26). The foolish man always believes he is right. He doesn't seek the advise of others. Hence, the fool doesn't really believe he can sin. This is want led to the downfall of Israel (Judges 17:6).

"Fools mock at sin, But among the upright there is favor" (Proverbs 14:9). Even when caught in sin, the fool will try to minimize the impact by saying that the sin wasn't really so bad. They will excuse themselves by pointing that others do the same thing. Some will go so far as to declare that the sin really isn't a sin. In the end, the fool makes a mockery of the seriousness of sin. Sin becomes a sport to the fool (Proverbs 10:23). Think about the young men who call fornication "scoring." Or, gambling institutions who want their wares to be called "gaming."

Without the belief that he can sin, the foolish man plows through life ignoring the signs of danger up ahead. "A prudent man foresees evil and hides himself, But the simple pass on and are punished" (Proverbs 22:3). The fool won't let such a minor thing as sin stop him from reaching for his goal.

Ultimately, a Fool Denies God

Because a fool refuses all restraint on his actions, he will ultimately turn against God. "The fool has said in his heart, "There is no God." They are corrupt, and have done abominable iniquity; There is none who does good"

(Psalm 53:1). They use their own standards and emotions to judge whether actions are right or wrong. They no longer consider God's thoughts on any matter. Soon God never enters their minds (Romans 1:20-22).

It is not that the evidence of God's existence is not available to them. The evidence is obvious, but to accept the evidence means to acknowledge that God is over them. Such men would much rather create gods to please their whims than to submit to the one, true God.

Why should any want to be such a fool?

Persuading Others of the Truth

Christianity is not blind following, but a reasoned decision. When we present the gospel to others, we need to persuade them of its advantages. *"For we must all appear before the judgment seat of Christ, that each one may receive the things done in the body, according to what he has done, whether good or bad. Knowing, therefore, the terror of the Lord, we persuade men; but we are well known to God, and I also trust are well known in your consciences"* (II Corinthians 5:10-11). This is what Paul did as he traveled:

"Now when the congregation had broken up, many of the Jews and devout proselytes followed Paul and Barnabas, who, speaking to them, <u>persuaded</u> them to continue in the grace of God" (Acts 13:43).

"Then Paul, as his custom was, went in to them, and for three Sabbaths <u>reasoned</u> with them from the Scriptures, <u>explaining</u> and <u>demonstrating</u> that the Christ had to suffer and rise again from the dead, and saying, "This Jesus whom I preach to you is the Christ." And some of them were <u>persuaded</u>; and a great multitude of the devout Greeks, and not a few of the leading women, joined Paul and Silas" (Acts 17:2-4).

"Now while Paul waited for them at Athens, his spirit was provoked within him when he saw that the city was given over to idols. Therefore he <u>reasoned</u> in the synagogue with the Jews and with the Gentile worshipers, and in the marketplace daily with those who happened to be there" (Acts 17:16-17).

"And he <u>reasoned</u> in the synagogue every Sabbath, and <u>persuaded</u> both Jews and Greeks" (Acts 18:4).

"And he went into the synagogue and spoke boldly for three months, <u>reasoning</u> and <u>persuading</u> concerning the things of the kingdom of God" (Acts 19:8).

"So when they had appointed him a day, many came to him at his lodging, to whom he <u>explained</u> and solemnly <u>testified</u> of the kingdom of God, <u>persuading</u> them concerning Jesus from both the Law of Moses and the Prophets, from morning till evening. And some were <u>persuaded</u> by the things which were spoken, and some disbelieved." (Acts 28:23).

The Art of Persuasion

Persuading others of the truth requires wisdom on the part of the teacher. He needs to know when to speak, what to speak, and how it needs to be spoken. *"Walk in wisdom toward those who are outside, redeeming the time. Let your speech always be with grace, seasoned with salt, that you may know how you ought to answer each one"* (Colossians 4:5-6). As with all wisdom, experience is the most effective teacher. You have to get out and talk with people about the gospel. Very quickly you will learn where there are holes in your knowledge. Hit the books and fill them in. Different people reason in different ways. When you run into an argument that throws you for a loop, sit back and analyze it. Is it proper reasoning or not? If it is faulty, where is the flaw that you can point out to others so they too can recognize the flaw?

Don't prejudge your audience. You never know who is going to respond to the gospel. Some of those whom I thought would never be interested turn out to be the strongest supporters of God's words. Others, whom I just knew would find the gospel appealing fall away rapidly. God wants everyone saved (I Timothy 2:3-4), so give everyone you meet an opportunity to respond to the gospel.

While illustrations are not proof, they do make grasping difficult concepts easier by relating the difficult to everyday events. Jesus used this method of teaching regularly, such as in his parables. One illustration that we often overlook is our own life. Things to which we can relate first-hand are far more persuasive than abstract ideas. This is to what Paul credited his ability to lead others to God. *"And I thank Christ Jesus our Lord who has enabled me, because He counted me faithful, putting me into the ministry, although I was formerly a blasphemer, a persecutor, and an insolent man; but I obtained mercy because I did it ignorantly in unbelief. And the grace of our Lord was exceedingly abundant, with faith and love which are in Christ Jesus. This is a faithful saying and worthy of all acceptance, that Christ*

Jesus came into the world to save sinners, of whom I am chief. However, for this reason I obtained mercy, that in me first Jesus Christ might show all longsuffering, as a pattern to those who are going to believe on Him for everlasting life" (I Timothy 1:12-16). Often we are too embarrassed to mention our past mistakes. Our pride prevents us from lowering ourselves in the sight of others. But people caught in the trap of sin need to see that it is possible to get out and what better way to show the possibility than with your own life.

Yet, remember that you cannot persuade others to the truth if you are unable to live by it. *"Let no one despise your youth, but be an example to the believers in word, in conduct, in love, in spirit, in faith, in purity. ... Meditate on these things; give yourself entirely to them, that your progress may be evident to all. Take heed to yourself and to the doctrine. Continue in them, for in doing this you will save both yourself and those who hear you"* (I Timothy 4:12, 15-16, see also Titus 2:7-8). Nothing ruins a good argument quicker than "Well, I don't see you doing that so why should I?"

Don't get so caught up in winning the argument that you lose sight of your goal of persuading. *"And a servant of the Lord must not quarrel but be gentle to all, able to teach, patient, in humility correcting those who are in opposition, if God perhaps will grant them repentance, so that they may know the truth, and that they may come to their senses and escape the snare of the devil, having been taken captive by him to do his will"* (II Timothy 2:24-26). Persuasion requires patience. What is obvious to you may not be obvious to another. They probably haven't spent as much time as you have considering the topic. Often there are important facts that they haven't learned, which are needed to understand the point you are trying to reach. We live in an impatient society. We want results immediately and if they don't come immediately we are ready to throw in the towel. Yet, if we keep in mind that our goal is to get people to heaven, then we will be willing to spend whatever time it takes to get people pass the difficulties they have encountered.

Often the greatest hindrance to persuading others is our own pride. We know we are right. We know they are wrong. So, we don't take the time to see things from the other person's viewpoint. But without knowledge of what that person truly thinks and why he thinks that way, how can you persuade him out of his incorrect thinking? I have met people who think they are teaching others by taunting them with the incorrect conclusions of their thinking or the contractions with the Scriptures to which they come. Taunting might serve a wake-up call – to shock a person out of the complacency of their position – but if that is all a person offers, it will simply lead to frustration and anger. Persuasion requires teaching a person the facts and reasoning needed to reach the proper conclusion.

It is our concern for the souls of our fellow men that should motivate us (II Corinthians 5:10-11). *"Remember that Jesus Christ, of the seed of David, was raised from the dead according to my gospel, for which I suffer trouble as an evildoer, even to the point of chains; but the word of God is not chained. Therefore I endure all things for the sake of the elect, that they also may obtain the salvation which is in Christ Jesus with eternal glory"* (II

Timothy 2:8-13). Unless you are fully convinced of the immense importance of your topic, you cannot effectively persuade others.

You must also realize your responsibility to teach others. Without a sense of duty, we will let opportunities slip by because it wasn't convenient. *"For if I preach the gospel, I have nothing to boast of, for necessity is laid upon me; yes, woe is me if I do not preach the gospel!"* (I Corinthians 9:16). Effective persuasion requires taking advantage of every opportunity to teach the message of God. *"Preach the word! Be ready in season and out of season. Convince, rebuke, exhort, with all longsuffering and teaching."* (II Timothy 4:2)

Teaching is a two-way street

While much can be learned from listening to a lecture, lectures may not be the most effective method of teaching in all cases. New ideas are being presented to the student which will naturally trigger questions as the student seeks to integrate the ideas into his way of thinking. At times the new ideas will conflict with old assumptions and this conflict must be resolved before the student is persuaded.

The effective teacher will be expecting questions. *"Always be ready to give a defense to everyone who asks you a reason for the hope that is in you, with meekness and fear"* (I Peter 3:15). This is not to say that you will have answers for every question or argument presented to you, but a good number of questions can be anticipated. Study the ones you can think of in advance.

Not every argument is worth a reply (II Timothy 2:23; Titus 3:9). Some get caught up in minor side issues which distract from the major goal of winning souls for Christ and getting them to their heavenly home. *"As I urged you when I went into Macedonia--remain in Ephesus that you may charge some that they teach no other doctrine, nor give heed to fables and endless genealogies, which cause disputes rather than godly edification which is in faith. Now the purpose of the commandment is love from a pure heart, from a good conscience, and from sincere faith, from which some, having strayed, have turned aside to idle talk, desiring to be teachers of the law, understanding neither what they say nor the things which they affirm"* (I Timothy 1:3-7). We are not to get caught up in wrestling over the meaning of words. *"Remind them of these things, charging them before the Lord not to strive about words to no profit, to the ruin of the hearers. Be diligent to present yourself approved to God, a worker who does not need to be ashamed, rightly dividing the word of truth. But shun profane and idle babblings, for they will increase to more ungodliness. And their message will spread like cancer"* (II Timothy 2:14-17). Keep your focus on the task at hand.

Methods of Persuasion

Example:
Personal example can often reach people who will not listen to words. *"Wives, likewise, be submissive to your own husbands, that even if some do not obey the word, they, without a word, may be won by the conduct of their*

wives, when they observe your chaste conduct accompanied by fear" (I Peter 3:1-2). We may tune out a person's words, but we can't help seeing a person's behavior.

Examples give others the encouragement to continue walking the path of righteousness (I Thessalonians 1:6-8). It greatly helps to know that God's way does work, that it can make a difference in a person's life (I Timothy 4:12; I Peter 2:21; Hebrews 12:1-3).

Of course, setting an example is not a complete method of teaching. It demonstrates one way that something may be accomplished, but it doesn't explain why it was done in that manner. Examples do not give the student the parameters needed to adjust behavior when they are faced with slight different circumstances. One of my favorite stories in Acts is of seven men who after observing Paul cast out demons decided they would do so as well (Acts 19:11-16). They said all the right words, but they were not obedient to the one in whose authority they attempted to cast out a demon.

Hence, examples teach a way to accomplish things. Examples gives encouragement to learn more. But, we can never expect to teach someone solely by example.

Lecture:

Lectures shine as a way to get a large quantity of information over to an audience in the shortest amount of time. Lectures were employed by Jesus, such as his sermon on the Mount in Matthew 5-7. Many of the sermons recorded for us in Acts are forms of lectures.

Ideally, lectures will trigger discussions, either in public or private, where those who heard the message of God can integrate the message with their own thoughts. Note in the gospels how often Jesus' speeches trigger questions from his audience or cause the disciples to approach him in private to ask a question that was bothering them.

Of course, lectures can only be effective if those in the audience are listening. It is very easy for people to tune out what you are saying. Again take note of Jesus' lessons in the gospels and notice how little impact his lessons made on the Pharisees and Sadducees in his audience. The fault did not lie with the Master Teacher, but with the unwilling students. *"And the disciples came and said to Him, 'Why do You speak to them in parables?' He answered and said to them, 'Because it has been given to you to know the mysteries of the kingdom of heaven, but to them it has not been given. For whoever has, to him more will be given, and he will have abundance; but whoever does not have, even what he has will be taken away from him. Therefore I speak to them in parables, because seeing they do not see, and hearing they do not hear, nor do they understand. And in them the prophecy of Isaiah is fulfilled, which says: 'Hearing you will hear and shall not understand, and seeing you will see and not perceive; for the hearts of this people have grown dull. Their ears are hard of hearing, and their eyes they have closed, lest they should see with their eyes and hear with their ears, lest they should understand with their hearts and turn, so that I should heal them.' But blessed are your eyes for they see, and your ears for they hear'"* (Matthew 13:10-16).

Group discussion:

Public discussion of questions can help many understand the nuances of the message. Here we can explore the range of possible applications and straighten out our own misconceptions. Yet, group discussions also have their limits. Some discussions become a pooling of ignorance instead of building of insight. In John 6:26-66 is the record of discussion Jesus had with a non-receptive crowd. While Jesus answered their questions, the answers triggered many side discussions among the audience. Rather than learning, they bolstered each one's ignorance. They complained that the teaching was too hard, giving themselves satisfaction that they had a right to reject Jesus' teaching because others also rejected it.

For public discussions to be effective, there must be one or more people who understand the truth. These people must ready and able to answer the questions and arguments presented in order to persuade others of the truth. Preferably the leader of the discussion must stay one step ahead of the group to show them the way they need to go. Otherwise, the conversation will splinter into numerous topics without any being fully addressed. This requires the leader of the discussion to have a goal in mind, a lesson that he wants to bring across, a point he wants made. Without a resolution, no progress is made in learning.

Debates are a form of group discussion, which will be discussed in greater detail in the next chapter.

Experience:

Some people seem unable to learn until they experience the lesson first-hand. Peter thought he would never deny the Lord until he was forced to learn that he was vulnerable (Matthew 26:31-35, 55-58, 69-75). For the teacher of truth, this can be difficult. The teacher sees the danger and knows the eventual outcome. He never desires harm for his student, but sometimes hurt makes the most lasting impression. Consider the parable of the prodigal son in Luke 15:11-32. When the younger son demanded his inheritance, his father gave it too him even though he surely knew it would come to a bad end. Yet, the father was ready to help his son pick up the pieces of his ruined life when the lesson finally sunk through his thick skull.

The danger with learning by experience is that at times the lesson is never learned. The danger overwhelms the student. The teacher should only willingly use experience when the outcome can be controlled. Yet, when a student insists on putting himself in harm's way, the teacher should not despair that all is lost. Hope remains that the stubborn student will learn his lesson from the school of hard-knocks and one day return. This is one of the motivations behind withdrawal from a sinner (I Corinthians 5:5; I Timothy 1:20).

Personal conversation:

Not everyone will have the patience to listen to a lecture, especially if they have not realized that the topic is vital to their life. And in group discussions some are too shy or too quiet to voice their questions; or, others so dominate the discussion that they are unable to get a word in edgewise. The teacher must cultivate personal relationships with each student so that opportunities arise to address personal questions and issues.

An oft cited text is the private discussion that Nicodemus had with Jesus that is recorded in John 3:1-21. It is likely that Nicodemus went to Jesus privately because he feared what others would think of him, but one of the results of that conversation was Nicodemus becoming a follower of Jesus (John 7:50; 19:39).

The disciples often saved some of their most direct questions for private conversations (Mark 4:34; 7:17). Aquila and Priscilla corrected the errors of Apollos privately resulting in a man who powerfully defended the truth (Acts 18:24-28).

Debates

"Where is the wise? Where is the scribe? Where is the disputer of this age? Has not God made foolish the wisdom of this world? For since, in the wisdom of God, the world through wisdom did not know God, it pleased God through the foolishness of the message preached to save those who believe" (I Corinthians 1:20-21).

At times I have run into people who argue against the use of public debates in the defense of the gospel. From their viewpoint, debates cause contentions between people and don't resolve disputes. Sometimes II Timothy 2:24-26 is cited where Paul said, *"a servant of the Lord must not quarrel."* The problem with this viewpoint is that it places Paul against himself. When faced with teachers attempting to bind the Law of Moses on Christians, *"Paul and Barnabas had great dissension and debate with them"* (Acts 15:2). Are we prepared to tell Paul that he was wrong to debate this issue with the Jewish Christians? Was it wrong for the church in Jerusalem to debate the issue as recorded in Acts 15:7?

The word which is translated as "debate" in several translations is the Greek word *suzetesis*. It, and the related words *suzeteo* and *suzetetes*, refer to sharp discussions, disputes, or questioning. When Jesus presented difficult points, it often resulted in debates among his listeners (Mark 1:27; 9:10). The two disciples Jesus met on the road to Emmaus were engaged in a debate (usually translated discussing, reasoning, or questioning) over recent events.

We also find debates occurring between believers and unbelievers. When the disciples were unable to cast out a demon, the scribes used the opportunity to debate them (Mark 9:14-29). Some Jews attempted to debate Stephen, but they could not match his wisdom (Acts 6:9-10). Jews of Greek origin also debated Paul with no better success (Acts 9:29). Apollos became an accomplished debater after his conversion (Acts 18:27-28).

Those who argue against debates fail to distinguish between reasoned arguments and strife. Strife is condemned in the Scriptures, but debates are accepted.

Strife

Paul instructs both Timothy and Titus repeatedly to avoid situations which lead to strife. It is an important topic for preachers since they often find themselves at odds with others. Even Christians who are not preachers can learn to be more selective about the things they choose to argue. All people in close relationships eventually have disagreements, but all disagreements are not worth battling over.

Foolish Disputes (I Timothy 6:4; II Timothy 2:23; Titus 3:9)

Controversy based on ignorance and illogic does not benefit anyone, Yet there are many who will engage in arguments without examining their stand. *"But avoid foolish and ignorant disputes, knowing that they generate strife"* (II Timothy 2:23). It is useless to engage such people in a debate since there is little with which to work. This is why the next verse tells Christians not to quarrel. You cannot reason with someone who is unreasonable or ignorant. You cannot properly defend a matter about which you know little.

Myths or Fables (I Timothy 1:4; 4:7; Titus 1:14)

In order to void churning in unproductive arguments, we must carefully choose the topics we will address. Make sure you have sufficient Scriptural basis before engaging in an argument. What use is it to argue over whether Jesus was born in April or August? It might be interesting to look as some of the evidence, but to hold that it must be one particular month is demanding more than what God has told us. I have heard people argue that those serving on the Lord's Table must wear a suit and tie. Another held the view that saying a prayer before the collection was unscriptural. Most of these topics are not worth debating because they are based upon personal opinion. *"As I urged you when I went into Macedonia--remain in Ephesus that you may charge some that they teach no other doctrine, nor give heed to fables and endless genealogies, which cause disputes rather than godly edification which is in faith"* (I Timothy 1:3-4). When arguments are not based on a standard, there is no method available to arrive at the truth.

Mosaical Law (Titus 3:9)

Since the Law of Moses has ended (Ephesians 2:14-15; Colossians 2:13-14; Hebrews 8:13), it would be a waste of time to argue about the subtle nuances of the Jewish law. There are things in the law which help our understanding of the law of Christ (Romans 15:4), but to argue about which sacrifice should be offered for a particular sin is not a productive use of time.

Commandments of Men (I Timothy 6:3; Titus 1:14)

Arguments about laws which men create is also a fruitless task. Man-made laws are based on individual standards and not the standards of God. For example, to argue whether priests should wear collars or not is not a practical use of your time. The New Testament does not recognize a special class of Christians called priests; all Christians are priests (I Peter 2:5,9). To argue about clothing requirements for a non-existent class of Christians is unproductive. Most Catholics view the Scriptures as one of several sources of authority. Catholics can prove their beliefs by citing sources outside of the Scriptures, but not necessarily from the Scriptures alone. A debate where each side proves his point by different standards is pointless.

Topics Which Have No Conclusion (I Timothy 1:4; Titus 3:9)

Some topics can never be fully settled because insufficient information is given to reach a final conclusion. Genealogies are a prime example of such topics. There are many genealogies given in the Bible and they serve a useful purpose; but we must remember that none of the genealogies are complete. For example, everyone has both a mother and a father, but most of the lineages in the Bible only follow one parent since they have a specific idea to prove. Some lineages have odd loops because people of different generations intermarry (try mapping out the Herod family sometime). To spend time arguing over fine points of genealogy is fruitless because it misses the whole point as to why the genealogies are given in the Scriptures. They do not exist for their own sake, but to prove greater points.

Other topics can fall into this same category. Arguing over the number of wings angels have or how many angels can dance on the head of a pin are classic examples. Some of the topics that Christians have argued for years actually revolve around what is not said in the Scriptures. To debate about differences over what is not said is unproductive. For example, one raging debate at the time of this writing revolves around "When does a divorce take place?" Some argue that it is when a person decides to divorce, others say it is when the divorce papers are filed, and still others say it is when the divorce is made final by a judge. The truth of the matter is that the Scriptures do not state what constitutes "putting away" a spouse. Hence, arguing over this detail is an argument that will never end.

Worldly Matters (I Timothy 4:7; 6:20; II Timothy 2:16)

Generally translated as "profane babblings," the word refers to things of a worldly origin. Many denominations are engaged in debates about whether to accept homosexuals as members of their clergy or whether living together before marriage should be called a sin. Such things are not up for debate because God clearly states

His position on sin. The sole reason it is being debated among the denominations is because of the acceptance of some of these sins by worldly people. The denominations believe they will gain more members if they display tolerance for certain practices. Such views are empty-headed nonsense and not worth the effort to debate. Instead, a solid "thus says the Lord" is more than sufficient.

Empty Talk (I Timothy 6:20; II Timothy 2:16)
Some people get caught up in arguments to which there is no point. I remember a Catholic priest wanted to discuss whether the grass was green on the hill where Jesus gave the sermon on the mount. His goal was to establish authority for extra-biblical sources, but the problem was that it really doesn't matter if the grass was green or brown from a drought. The condition of the grass does not change the meaning of Jesus' words. I have had more than one person want to argue whether the cross Jesus died upon was "t" shaped or a straight pole. My response has always been, "What difference will it make if we settle on a shape?" Usually I am told, "none," but they still want to argue the point.

Arguments over empty words only serve to divide people and to keep Christians from using their time productively and addressing real issues.

Strife About Words (I Timothy 6:4; II Timothy 2:14)
Sometimes we lose our focus over the issues between ourselves and others and we spend more time arguing who's dictionary is right than what is right. The meaning

of words is important, but ultimately we must realize that dictionaries are extra-biblical sources. Fortunately, most definitions can be established by the context in which they are used. The vast majority of dictionaries agree on most words. Yet many people will take firm stances on meanings they do not have the background to judge.

As an example, many Jehovah Witnesses have reference books which give the wrong definition to the word "earth" in II Peter 3:10. To enter into a debate where they appeal to their reference material and you appeal to your reference material is a debate that will not be settled. Since both reference works are works of men, there will be no conclusion. However, if you appeal to how the word is used in other contexts within the Scriptures, you may be able to persuade others of the truth.

Contentious People (I Timothy 6:3-5; Titus 3:9)
Christians must also be aware that some are not interested in promoting the truth, they are only interested in promoting themselves. Such people use arguments as an attempt to draw more followers to themselves.

Similarly, there are people who enjoy arguing for the sake of arguing. They will take a contrary stand simply to stir up strife. Their enjoyment comes from the clashing of ideas and not from locating the truth.

Contrary People (I Timothy 6:20-21; Titus 3:10-11)
There are also people who take delight in finding fault instead of finding the truth. They will spend hours searching for supposed contradictions. While Christians

must always be ready to defend the truth, we must realize that skeptics are not interested in the truth. The Christian should answer, but not argue because the arguments will never cease.

Debate

"The first one to plead his cause seems right, until his neighbor comes and examines him" (Proverbs 18:17). There is a natural advantage to the first speaker in a debate. Yet if the truth is being sought, all sides of a matter must be considered. When some argued that Christians had to be circumcised and follow the law of Moses, the leaders of the church looked into the matter and spent time debating the issue before arriving at their conclusion (Acts 15:5-7).

Issues must be clearly defined if a productive discussion is going to take place. In formal debates, the two parties makes statements that affirm or deny an issue. Often games are played in establishing those statements. A good debate can take place when the difference is clearly expressed. Ideally, the affirmative statement is something the person believes is true. The denial statement is something a person believes is false. For example, we could affirm that "Baptism by immersion saves a person" and deny that "Baptism by sprinkling or pouring brings salvation to a person." The issue then is the difference in how baptism is administered. Some debaters, to put their opponent in an awkward position, will insist that they affirm the negative of what they deny. Using the same example, to affirm that "A person who is sprinkled or poured upon is not saved" and to deny that "A person can be saved without being immersed" is more difficult to defend. At first they appear to be the similar stances, but consider this: Was Abraham saved by baptism? You see the double negative hides broad interpretations.

Many of the positions that Christians affirm are not denied by people in the denominations. I don't know anyone who will say that a baptized believer is not saved. They will say that baptism is not necessary, but they will not claim that it is harmful. Hence, to keep any debate productive, whether formal or informal, the difference must be clearly expressed. Without a clear understanding of where we stand, we can easily be pulled into idle talk. *"Now the purpose of the commandment is love from a pure heart, from a good conscience, and from sincere faith, from which some, having strayed, have turned aside to idle talk, desiring to be teachers of the law, understanding neither what they say nor the things which they affirm"* (I Timothy 1:5-7).

Proper defense of the Gospel requires men who are not angered by poorly expressed positions. *"But avoid foolish and ignorant disputes, knowing that they generate strife. And a servant of the Lord must not quarrel but be gentle to all, able to teach, patient, in humility correcting those who are in opposition, if God perhaps will grant them repentance, so that they may know the truth, and that they may come to their senses and escape the snare of the devil, having been taken captive by him to do his will"* (II Timothy 2:23-26). The goal of all debates is to instruct – either the one being debated or the audience watching the debate. In either case, anger does not productively instruct other people (James 1:20).

It is very tempting to bolster you case by tearing down your opponent. Usually people will stoop to this tactic when they feel they are in a poor position, as the Pharisees did to the blind man in John 9:24. But I have seen people with solid positions do the same. Such is not proper. Paul tells us *"to speak evil of no one, to be peaceable, gentle, showing all humility to all men"* (Titus 3:2). It does not matter who is right, but what is right. Far too many preachers and debaters spend more time attacking the character of their opponent than dealing with the issue of disagreement.

Proof in a debate must be offered from a common source that all agree is authoritative. For Christians defending the gospel, our source is the Bible. *"If anyone speaks, let him speak as the oracles of God"* (I Peter 4:11). A solid, logical use of the Scriptures is hard to avoid. *"For the weapons of our warfare are not carnal but mighty in God for pulling down strongholds, casting down arguments and every high thing that exalts itself against the knowledge of God, bringing every thought into captivity to the obedience of Christ"* (II Corinthians 10:4-5). If we place our confidence in the word of God, we will not find ourselves cornered in an indefensible position.

The writer of Proverbs warns, *"Do not answer a fool according to his folly, lest you also be like him. Answer a fool according to his folly, lest he be wise in his own eyes"* (Proverbs 26:4-5). At first glance, the two statements appear to be contradictory, but they are not and the difference is important. When responding to a foolish argument in a debate, do not respond by making the same mistake. If it is dumb for him, then it will not improve when you use the same method. At the same time, an opponent should be treated as he acts. An opponent who makes reasoned, though incorrect arguments should be treated with respect. But an opponent who makes silly responses should have his lack of reasoning exposed, even though it may embarrass him before others. As an example, I once had a fellow argue that baptism took place under the Old Testament. Since the Old Testament is no longer in effect, then baptism is no longer in effect. My response was in kind. David prayed while living under the Old Testament Law. Since the Old Testament is no longer in effect, are you willing to say that prayer is not in effect under Christ's law. The answer was so embarrassingly obvious the gentleman refused to discuss the matter further.

Effective Rebukes

"It is better to hear the rebuke of the wise than for a man to hear the song of fools." (Ecclesiastes 7:5)

Few Christians enjoy confrontations. We desire peace and harmony, so we avoid displays of disagreement as much as possible. Yet, it is easy to go too far in avoiding conflicts. Satan's influence remains in the world. If we do not take a stand against evil, then evil wins. All Satan needs to further his cause is for Christians to do nothing. We cannot be timid about doing things we don't like to do (II Timothy 1:7).

It is a fact of our lives that we all make mistakes. None of us are perfect and we all will commit sins from time to time (Romans 3:9-23). A person on the path of sin needs his course corrected, whether he is unaware of the sin or ignoring its harmful influence in his life. A rebuke is required to make a person aware of his need to change his life.

While all Christians should be able to rebuke someone in error, rebuking is a duty assigned to elders and preachers. Elders must be *"able, by sound doctrine, both to exhort and convict those who contradict"* (Titus 1:9). Preachers are to *"Preach the word! Be ready in season and out of season. Convince, rebuke, exhort, with all longsuffering and teaching"* (II Timothy 4:2). These men have the authority of God given to them to perform this duty and it is not to be ignored (Titus 2:15). This is not to say that elders and preachers are the dictators of a congregation. They have no authority to make up rules for the church. However, when they see a fellow Christian straying from the laws of Christ, it is their duty to see that Christ's laws are upheld.

When people neglect to rebuke those who are straying from the truth, it gives falsehood the opportunity to spread. *"For there are many insubordinate, both idle talkers and deceivers, especially those of the circumcision, whose mouths must be stopped, who subvert whole households, teaching things which they ought not, for the sake of dishonest gain"* (Titus 1:10-11). Uncorrected problems never shrink, they grow until they sweep whole congregations away from the truth. *"Do you not know that a little leaven leavens the whole lump? Therefore purge out the old leaven, that you may be a new lump"* (I Corinthians 5:6-7). Even in the Old Testament, God complained that the Israelite leaders were silent dogs; they were unable to give warning when danger approached and so Israel became corrupted by sin (Isaiah 56:10-11).

Three Levels of Rebukes

There are three main words used to in connection with rebuking another. The Greek word *noutheteo* means to caution or gently reprove. It is often translated as admonished or warn. It is used in regards to preachers and elders warning people (Colossians 1:28, I Thessalonians 5:12) or Christians admonishing each other in song (Colossians 3:16). The Greek word *elegcho* refers to convincing a person of his fault. It is generally translated convict, rebuke, or reprove. It is used of convincing the wicked they are in sin (Ephesians 5:11, 13; Titus 1:9) or reproving elders publicly for their unrepented sins (I Timothy 5:20). Finally, the Greek word *epitimao* means to censure or forbid. It is usually translated as rebuke or charge. It is the specific charge to preachers to rebuke when needed (II Timothy 4:2). All Christians are charged to rebuke a brother who sins (Luke 17:3).

How to Rebuke Effectively

It should go without saying that Christians should always stick to the truth (Ephesians 4:25). Frequently we become upset with people for what we assume they are thinking instead of what we know they are doing. We tend to ascribe motivations to a person's action, but we need to realize that only God knows the mind of other people (Hebrews 4:12-13). It is true that wrongful action originates from wrongful thoughts (Matthew 15:18-19), but unless the offender admits to why he is doing wrong, we must stick to rebuking the wrongful deeds. *"If your brother sins against you, rebuke him"* (Luke 17:3).

The standard of truth is the Scriptures. Since most people assume they are right, few based their rebukes upon the teachings in the Scriptures. The Pharisees are remembered for scolding Jesus' disciples for eating without washing their hands, but such a law is not found in the Scriptures (Matthew 15:1-3). God's laws are profitable as the basis of reproof (II Timothy 3:16-17), not laws of human origin.

When we show partiality for or against a person, let us say because of the way they dress or their nationality, we become judges with evil motives (James 2:4). We have a different agenda than seeing that a person lives righteously before God. When we deliver a rebuke, it must be done because it will better the person (Colossians 1:28-29; Titus 1:13).

Rebukes must also be given for the benefit of others who hear of the rebuke. Sin left uncorrected spreads (I Corinthians 5:6). At times even elders might sin and those who refuse to leave their sins are to be publicly rebuked by a preacher. *"Those who are sinning rebuke in the presence of all, that the rest also may fear"* (I Timothy 5:20).

When delivering rebukes, the Israelites were warned not to do so from hatred (Leviticus 19:17). The psalmist noted that when the righteous chasten, it is a kindness to the one being chastened (Psalm 141:5). Not that being corrected is enjoyable, but when you know that a good man is doing it for your own good, it is more tolerable. *"Now no chastening seems to be joyful for the present, but painful; nevertheless, afterward it yields the peaceable fruit of righteousness to those who have been trained by it"* (Hebrews 12:11). Rebuke wrong action, but do not attack the person's character. When a Christian is caught up in sin, he is to be admonished (gently corrected or cautioned) as a brother (II Thessalonians 3:15). Older men are to be treated respectfully, so sharp rebukes are to be avoided (I Timothy 5:1). As God told the Israelites, *"You shall rise before the gray headed and honor the presence of an old* man, and fear your God: I am the LORD" (Leviticus 19:32).

Rebukes should always be balanced with encouragement. If everything you say is always negative, people will come to dread your presence. We should not make a hobby of condemning others. *"Brethren, if a man is overtaken in any trespass, you who are spiritual restore such a one in a spirit of gentleness, considering yourself lest you also be tempted. Bear one another's burdens, and so fulfill the law of Christ"* (Galatians 6:1-2). One way to keep a proper perspective is to note the positive points a person has before you tell them what they are currently doing wrong.

Because of our general reluctance to correct a person, we sometimes procrastinate until so many things have gone wrong that we can no longer tolerate it. Then we let the person have it with everything they have done wrong in the past. The problem with this approach is that it overwhelms the person. He tends to block out everything that you say; and so, little or nothing is actually corrected. Paul tells us that love keeps no records of wrongs (I Corinthians 13:5). One way to accomplish this is to address problems as they happen, one problem at a time. Parents quickly learn they cannot give complex instructions to children because they forget and end up accomplishing nothing. The same rule needs to be used when correcting bad behavior. Address one issue at a time and it will more likely be addressed.

In a similar vein, correction should be given as soon after the wrong behavior as possible. The longer you delay, the less effective the correction because the bad behavior will have become ingrained in the person. This is one reason why Paul warned, "'*Be angry, and do not sin*': *do not let the sun go down on your wrath, nor give place to the devil*" (Ephesians 4:26-27). A major reason most congregations are unable bring erring members out of sin is because they delay addressing problems for months or sometimes even years.

Good and Bad Rebukes

A wife may complain to her husband, "We don't go out very often." It is a general statement of fact that leaves the reason why they are not getting out wide open. The statement doesn't assign blame but points out a problem that needs to be addressed. A poor way to approach the same problem would be to say, "You never take me anywhere." With the latter statement full blame is placed on the person. The problem itself takes a backseat. The latter statement is also an over-generalization. Few couples *never* leave the house together. The person on the receiving end of this rebuke will feel obligated to defend himself. Since it is not a fair representation of the situation, the true problem is not addressed.

A parent may say, "There are dirty dishes in the sink when I came home. We had agreed this morning that you would wash them." Here, once again, the focus is placed on the problem. Contrast this to "You left dirty dishes in the sink *again*. You promised you wouldn't. I just can't trust you, can I?" In the latter statement, the current problem is overshadowed by past problems. Instead of waiting to learn the reason for the neglect, the child's character is attacked and a prejudgement is given that the child is unworthy of future trust. The child receiving the former rebuke has an opportunity to explain what happened. The child receiving the latter rebuke will feel that there is no reason to reply because the decision has already been made.

Another complain might be, "I was expecting you to come straight home. You didn't even call." Notice that the focus is on what happened. The speaker doesn't assign a reason as to why it happened, thereby inviting a discussion of the problem. Suppose the following was said instead, "You never think to call and tell me you'll be late. You always leave me hanging. You care more about your friends than me." Now the person's character is prejudged – he doesn't think and he has the wrong priorities. In addition the past is being brought up and over-generalized. Once again, the person receiving the later complaint will focus on defending his character and not address the problem at hand.

Responses to Rebukes

Rebukes are necessary, but they are rarely enjoyable. Godly people will struggle with their dislike of being criticized and will make an effort to learn from the rebuke. *"Rebuke is more effective for a wise man than a hundred blows on a fool"* (Proverbs 17:10). Afterwards, when there is a chance to look back, most people hold a grudging admiration for the one who gave an honest rebuke (Proverbs 28:23). "Yes men" are ever present looking for ways to use you to their advantage. When we want an honest assessment, we'll seek out someone who will point out our flaws along with our strengths. Honest rebukes will make us look better in the long run (Proverbs 25:12).

The wicked, of course, hate rebuke. They do not want their sins pointed out because they would rather believe their actions are not sins (Proverbs 13:1). As a result, the scoffer will not seek out the wise for advice because he is not interested in an honest assessment (Proverbs 15:12; 1:25, 30). If a person does try to rebuke a wicked person, the typical response is a personal hatred for the one delivering the rebuke. *"He who corrects a scoffer gets shame for himself, And he who rebukes a wicked man only harms himself. Do not correct a scoffer, lest he hate you; Rebuke a wise man, and he will love you"* (Proverbs 9:7-8). As Amos pointed out, *"They hate the one who rebukes in the gate, and they abhor the one who speaks uprightly"* (Amos 5:10). This is the reason the prophets were killed in the past (Nehemiah 9:26). The death of Stephen well illustrates the hatred the wicked have for those who rebuke theirs sins (Acts 7:51-58).

Sometimes when a person is rebuked he responds by hiding his faults instead of correcting them (Proverbs 19:25). Progress appears to have been made on the surface, but instead the problems are hidden under additional layers of deceit.

Some hate rebuke because they hate themselves (Proverbs 15:31-32). They already feel guilty about their sins and they hate being reminded of them. Their sins have been swept under the rug without correction. Because they are out of sight, they can pretend that they do not exist, so long as certain people do not provide reminders.

When the rebuke is towards someone else, people are more fair minded. They want the wicked corrected. They desire that justice is done. *"He who says to the wicked, "You are righteous," him the people will curse; nations will abhor him. But those who rebuke the wicked will have delight, and a good blessing will come upon them"* (Proverbs 24:24-25).

Public Rebukes

At times objections are made in regards to how a rebuke is delivered. Especially when on the receiving end, a person will argue that all rebukes must first be done privately and cite Matthew 18:15-18. What is overlooked is that Jesus was discussing how to deal with a private dispute between two brothers. In general the principle is that least number of people who need to know about a problem in order to get it resolved, the better. In Matthew 18:15-18, others are not aware of the problem between brothers until they are called in to witness. The church is not aware of the problem until the brothers and the witnesses bring it to the church's attention. But we must remember that not all problems are of a private nature. When Paul and Barnabas encountered false teaching, they publically disputed the claims of the false teachers (Acts 15:1-2). When Ananias lied before the church, he was rebuked before the church (Acts 5:1-5). When a man sinned so that the entire community knew of the sin, the church was commanded to withdraw from him immediately (I Corinthians 5:1-5).

Similarly, public rebukes are sometimes required when the sinning person holds a position of reputation and refuses to leave his sin. *"Do not receive an accusation against an elder except from two or three witnesses. Those who are sinning rebuke in the presence of all, that the rest also may fear"* (I Timothy 5:19-20).

In all cases, the need for public rebukes is to both change the sinner and to create a fear to sin in those who witness or hear about the rebuke. People who see others getting away with sins will soon justify their own misdeeds. But when a consistent standard is enforced, people will be less inclined to excuse their own actions. To keep public sins from spreading, it must be addressed in a public manner.

Questions:
1) Locate, if you can, passages where a public sin is dealt with privately.
2) Is there ever a case where a public sin is better dealt with privately?
3) Around 2000, the Roman Catholic church came under pressure for how they dealt with priests who had committed sexual sins. Why did their method of dealing with such sins privately not solve their problems?

Keeping the Context

"Be diligent to present yourself approved to God, a worker who does not need to be ashamed, rightly dividing the word of truth." (II Timothy 2:15)

Throughout the history of the church, odd ideas have been justified by means of Scriptures pulled out of context. For example, the Church of Jesus Christ of the Latter Day Saints (commonly called Mormons), use proxy baptism on behalf of ancestors who have died. Their justification is I Corinthians 15:29, *"Otherwise, what will they do who are baptized for the dead, if the dead do not rise at all? Why then are they baptized for the dead?"* The popular idea that salvation is by faith alone comes from citing passages which connect faith with salvation, such as John 3:16. The problem is that lack of context often makes a passage appear to say things not intended. For example, Jesus said, *"You are My friends if you do whatever I command you"* (John 15:14). Jesus told Judas, *"What you do, do quickly"* (John 13:27). Judas, we are told, *"departed, and went and hanged himself"* (Matthew 27:5). Finally, Jesus said, *"Go and do likewise"* (Luke 10:37). By selectively using quotes, we arrive at a conclusion that we know is incorrect – that Jesus wants followers to commit suicide.

Since nearly anything could be justified by the Bible if the context is ignored, it is important for the Christian to check any conclusion about a passage against the context of the Scripture. Even though we complain about others ignoring the context of a passage, we do our Lord disservice if we commit the same error while trying to defend the truth.

Peter warns, *"... our beloved brother Paul, according to the wisdom given to him, has written to you, as also in all his epistles, speaking in them of these things, in which are some things hard to understand, which untaught and unstable people twist to their own destruction, as they do also the rest of the Scriptures. You therefore, beloved, since you know this beforehand, beware lest you also fall from your own steadfastness, being led away with the error of the wicked"* (II Peter 3:15-17). The word translated "twist" in this passage comes from the Greek word for torturing a victim on a rack. The ignorant and unstable people of this world are quite willing to torture the meaning of a passage to justify their agenda. We must be on our guard so as to not fall into their dangerous thinking.

For example, the People for the Ethical Treatment of Animals (PETA) has published papers in 1999 claiming that Jesus was a vegetarian. Their proof? They point to Genesis 1:29-30 to claim that God's intention was a vegetarian world. They point to Jesus driving out the merchants from the temple in John 2:14-16 to claim that Jesus was saving animals from sacrifices and being eaten. Finally, they claim that no passage mentions Jesus eating meat.

Another example is an article written by Debra Haffner in 1997 titled "The Really Good News: What the Bible

Says About Sex." In this article, the author claims that David and Jonathan were homosexual lovers by citing II Samuel 1:26, I Samuel 18:1, and I Samuel 19:1. She also claims, the Song of Solomon, "does not talk about sex in the context of marriage or procreation: the woman in the Song is never 'called a wife, nor is she required to bear children. In fact, to the issue of marriage and procreation, the Song does not speak.'" Hence, she concludes that sex outside of marriage is approved. She also claims that "prostitution was an accepted part of urban society during biblical times (see I Kings 22:38; Isaiah 23:16; Proverbs 7:12, and 9:14)."

Most of us find these claims outrageous, but that is because we are familiar with the overall context of the Bible. While these examples are more blatantly false, many religious doctrine is also based on passages taken out of their appropriate context.

The Harmony of the Scriptures

Hermeneutics is the study of how to understand meaning of the written word. One basic principle in hermeneutics is the general assumption that every author's writings are in harmony, unless it is clearly established to be otherwise. We assume that an author writes in order to be understood. Hence, we would expect consistency in the author's message. Each writing of an author will contain a theme, or a purpose, to which the points in the message support. It is upon this principle that criminologists examine letters to determine if they are from the same individual or the work of a copycat. In his book *Principles of Interpretation*, Clinton Lockhart states, "One of two contradictory statements must be false, unless corresponding terms have different meanings or applications." In other words, if you have two statements that contradict, either the two statements are not from the same author, or the terms in the two statements are being used in different ways and with different meanings.

When hermeneutics is applied to the Scriptures, this general principle of harmony in meaning becomes an absolute. Men make mistakes, but the work of the all-knowing, all-mighty God cannot contain contradictions. God doesn't make mistakes. Hence, when we run into an apparent contradiction in the Bible, we must examine the context of the statements to see if there are terms being used in different senses of meaning or application.

Jesus used this principle when Satan tempted him in the wilderness. "*Then the devil took Him up into the holy city, set Him on the pinnacle of the temple, and said to Him, "If You are the Son of God, throw Yourself down. For it is written: 'He shall give His angels charge over you,' and, 'In their hands they shall bear you up, Lest you dash your foot against a stone.'" Jesus said to him, "It is written again, 'You shall not tempt the LORD your God.'"*"(Matthew 4:5-7). Satan quoted Psalm 91:11-12 where God promises protection, but Jesus countered with Deuteronomy 6:16 with the introductory words, "*It is written again.*" By pointing out an additional verse that appears to contradict the interpretation given to another verse, Jesus won the argument by showing that Satan made an error. Psalm 91:11-12 must be in harmony with

Deuteronomy 6:16 since God wrote both passages. Since the meaning Satan ascribed to Psalm 91:11-12 was not in harmony with Deuteronomy 6:16, Satan must have assigned the wrong meaning to the passage in Psalm.

Application in the Scriptures

How many angels were at the tomb after Jesus' resurrection? Matthew 28:1-3 mentions one, but Luke 24:1-4 mentions two. Skeptics are quick to pounce on this difference and declare that the Scriptures contradict one another and, therefore, are not inspired. Yet, consider this: Suppose I related an event that happened in a meeting and mentioned that brother John said something important. Would it be reasonable to conclude that only I and brother John met? Of course not! In the same manner, if Matthew mentions the appearance of an angel and records what that angel said, does this preclude the presence of additional angels? The answer remains, of course not! Why are there differences in the details recorded in Matthew and in Luke? It is due to the different purposes the two authors had in writing their respective books.

When Romans 4:5 is held up against James 2:24, we cannot state that the two authors contradicted each other. To so claim would be claiming that the message in one or both of the books is not inspired. Instead we need to examine the context of the two passages to see how the terms are being used. In particular, we need to see if the terms are being used with a different sense of meaning or application.

Both verses mention faith. Are there multiple faiths? Most realize that the faith exhibited by demons, mentioned in James 2:19, is different from the faith discussed in Hebrews 11:6, even though what is being believed is the same in both verses. When we examine the context of James, we realize that James' point is that the faith of demons is missing an essential element that causes it to be a useless faith.

Since Romans 4:5 and James 2:24 both mention works, we must also ask "Are there multiple works?" A quick glance through the New Testament shows us that there are:

- Works of God (John 6:28-29; 9:3-4).
- Works of the devil (I John 3:8),
- Works of man's hands (Acts 7:41),
- Works of the Law (Romans 3:20,27-28; Galatians 2:16),
- Good works (Ephesians 2:10; I Timothy 2:9-10), and
- Dead works (Hebrews 6:1).

Because both faith and works can take on different meanings in different contexts, we cannot make a blanket statement concerning faith or works without defining the kind of faith and the kind of work we are considering.

When we mention that baptism saves, as stated in I Peter 3:21, many object and hold up John 3:16. Yet, their very line of argument is in error. All that is being claimed is "my favorite verse is better than your favorite verse!" The reality is that all verses in the Bible come from one God. As Jesus pointed out to Satan, you cannot use a select set of verses against the rest of the Bible's teachings. Unfortunately, the denominational world does not look to harmonize the Scriptures. Instead, they search high and low for ways to dismiss the verses that do not agree with their preconceived notions. There must be an understanding of I Peter 3:21 and John 3:16 which allows both baptism and faith to save. Anything less is a declaration that the Scriptures contain contradictions and are not, therefore, inspired.

In order to understand God's Holy Word, we must be willing to seek the harmony of what is stated. We cannot pull a passage out of its context because the context defines how the words are being used. We cannot pit one passage against another without denying the inspiration of the Scriptures (Psalm 119:160; II Timothy 3:16-17).

Which context?

Immediate Context

Quotes should be used in the same manner in which the original passage was used. As an example, in the "justification" of suicide given above, Jesus is quoted as saying *"Go and do likewise"* in Luke 10:37. The usage implies that Jesus is telling us to do the same as Judas. But the reality is that Jesus was discussing the Law of Moses with a lawyer who wanted to play word games with the term "neighbor" (Luke 10:25-29). When Jesus proved that everyone is a man's neighbor he told the lawyer to *"go and do likewise"* – meaning to go and treat everyone as his neighbor.

Similar errors can be made by juxtaposing two passages discussing different topics to give the impression that they are discussing the same topic. One author made the following claim: "Jesus came to 'seek and save' only 'the lost sheep of the house of Israel' (Matthew 1:21; 2:6; 15:24; Luke 19:10)." The phrase "seek and save" comes from Luke 19:10 where Jesus stated he came to seek and save that which was lost. However, there is no limit in Luke 19:10 that the lost was only the lost in Israel. The phrase "the lost sheep of the house of Israel" comes from Matthew 15:24 where Jesus tells a Gentile woman, who was asking Jesus to heal her daughter, that he was only sent to the lost sheep of the house of Israel. Even in this context, Jesus did not mean he could not do miracles for the Gentiles because he proceeds to heal this woman's daughter. Instead, Jesus is simply explaining that the focus of his mission was only toward Israel. But the author of the quote combines a passage dealing with salvation and a passage about focus of mission to make a claim that neither passage supports.

Book Context

Each book in the Bible has a stated purpose and is directed to a particular audience. Any meaning assigned to a passage quoted from a book must be in harmony with the overall purpose of the book. For example, Seventh-Day Adventist pull passages from the Law of Moses to justify their worship services being on the Sabbath day (the seventh day of the week). Quoting one of the Ten Commandments and applying it to Christian violates the context of the book. The lead-in to the Ten

Commandments states *"The LORD our God made a covenant with us in Horeb. The LORD did not make this covenant with our fathers, but with us, those who are here today, all of us who are alive"* (Deuteronomy 5:2-3). Further, in discussing the Laws, Moses stated, *"For what great nation is there that has God so near to it, as the LORD our God is to us, for whatever reason we may call upon Him? And what great nation is there that has such statutes and righteous judgments as are in all this law which I set before you this day?"* (Deuteronomy 4:7-8). Obviously, the laws, including the Ten Commandments, were intended for the nation of Israel. They were not given to any other people prior, nor were they given to any other nation. To apply them now would be a violation of the context in which the book was presented.

Similar contextual errors are frequently made regarding the book of Revelation. Many fanciful ideas concerning the present times and near-future are based on passages pulled from Revelation. Yet the book of Revelation was written near the end of the first century and concerning his book, John wrote, *"The Revelation of Jesus Christ, which God gave Him to show His servants--things which must shortly take place. ... Blessed is he who reads and those who hear the words of this prophecy, and keep those things which are written in it; for the time is near"* (Revelation 1:1, 3). Jumping to the end of the book, the time frame of the book is again mentioned. *"And the Lord God of the holy prophets sent His angel to show His servants the things which must shortly take place"* (Revelation 22:6). While the future might be mentioned in the book, the overall contents of the book deals with events that would soon take place after the writing of the book. To assign twenty-first century meaning to a first or second century targeted book is a violation of the context.

Bible Context

Paul told the Corinthians that God does not author confusion (I Corinthians 14:33). He does not tell one person one thing and another something different. A young prophet learned this the hard way. The prophet was told to deliver a pronouncement against King Jeroboam and then return without eating or drinking (I Kings 13:16-17). An old prophet, who wanted the man as a guest claimed, *"I too am a prophet as you are, and an angel spoke to me by the word of the LORD, saying, 'Bring him back with you to your house, that he may eat bread and drink water'"*(I Kings 13:18). The young prophet lost his life because he did not understand that God does not change His commands and this prophet was lying to him.

It was to this consistency of God's message to which Paul appealed. *"I marvel that you are turning away so soon from Him who called you in the grace of Christ, to a different gospel, which is not another; but there are some who trouble you and want to pervert the gospel of Christ. But even if we, or an angel from heaven, preach any other gospel to you than what we have preached to you, let him be accursed. As we have said before, so now I say again, if anyone preaches any other gospel to you than what you have received, let him be accursed"* (Galatians

1:6-9). Hence an understanding of one verse that causes a conflict with another passage is not an understand, but a misunderstanding. It may take deeper study, but all of God's message is a unified message.

Handling contextual problems

When a passage can be interpreted in a variety of ways, it is helpful to make a list of all possible meanings. Then take your Bible and examine the immediate context, the book's context, and the Bible's context to see if any of the possible meanings conflict with the context. If they do, then you can eliminate that possibility. Often you will find yourself with only one possibility left.

As an illustration, take a verse that has caused difficulties for many ever since Paul wrote it, "*Otherwise, what will they do who are baptized for the dead, if the dead do not rise at all? Why then are they baptized for the dead?*" (I Corinthians 15:29). What is meant by "baptized for the dead?" Make a list of the of all the possible meanings that you can including the outlandish ones.

Here are several that I have heard
1. Paul is talking about being baptized for Christ, who had died for our sins.
2. People are being baptized to be numbered among the dead.
3. Paul is asking rhetorical questions. Baptism is supposed to bring life. If there is no resurrection, there is no future life, so those baptized are being baptized into the realm of the dead. Hence, Paul is pointing out

the paradox of practicing baptism while denying the resurrection.

4. People can be baptized on behalf of others who had already died.

5. Since Paul uses the third person "they," he is referring to a heretical sect that practiced baptism for people who had already died.

6. The phrase "for the dead" can be rendered "on account of the dead," thus Paul is discussing people who are following the example people who have died before them or a desire to join loved ones who were Christians but are now dead. In other words, the phrase speaks of the motivation for being baptized. Hence, Paul is arguing why continue to practice baptism when the motivation is removed because of a denial of a resurrection.

7. People are being baptized to take the place of those who have died; thereby, they are keeping Christianity alive.

First, we need to consider the immediate context of the passage. Whatever the practice under discussion, Paul is using it in a favorable sense to prove that there must be a resurrection from the dead. Truth cannot be proven from error. If Paul was referring to a Corinthian practice which he did not approve, why wasn't it rebuked as all the other erroneous practices mentioned in the letter? Hence, the immediate context eliminates the heretical sect argument (#5).

In the immediate context, we can also examine the word "dead" and find that it is a plural noun in the Greek. The dead refers to a group of people and not a single person. This eliminates the argument that Paul is referring to Christ (#1).

Since Paul is using this baptism to argue for the resurrection, it would be strange to claim that people are being baptized to be numbered among the dead. As Paul argued in Romans 6:4, baptism is to bring life. Hence by immediate context and biblical context, argument #2 is wrong. Similarly, while there is nothing wrong with the idea that Christians would continue to spread the gospel, bringing in new people to replace those who have passed on, the idea does not further Paul's argument that there must be a resurrection. Hence, we eliminate #7 as a possibility.

If we continue to examine the biblical context, we see that God has always made men responsible for their own actions. In Ezekiel 18:20 we read, *"The soul who sins shall die. The son shall not bear the guilt of the father, nor the father bear the guilt of the son. The righteousness of the righteous shall be upon himself, and the wickedness of the wicked shall be upon himself."* Even though Jesus died for us while we were sinners, God still requires sinners to respond to the invitation to be saved. Dead people cannot repent. They cannot respond. This is why there is an urgency to teach the gospel while people are still living. *"For we must all appear before the judgment seat of Christ, that each one may receive the things done in the body, according to what he has done, whether good or bad"* (II Corinthians 5:10). Hence, being baptized in substitution for the dead (#4) is not true.

Who then are the "they" in verse 29? It is a reference back to the group mentioned in verse 12. There were people in Corinth who were denying the resurrection. Paul is wondering why they are practicing baptism and why he and others were placing their lives in jeopardy (verse 30) if there was no resurrection.

While we might not firmly establish exactly what Paul meant by his statement in I Corinthians 15:29, the use of context does narrow down the possibilities quickly and allows for more reasoned discussion.

Questions
1) List other possible meanings for I Corinthians 15:29.
2) Using the context, which possible meanings are eliminated?

Reasoning Without Truth

"But we have renounced the hidden things of shame, not walking in craftiness nor handling the word of God deceitfully, but by manifestation of the truth commending ourselves to every man's conscience in the sight of God" (II Corinthians 4:2).

You can prove anything when you start with a falsehood. If I presented made-up evidence I could use the imaginary "proof" to justify a false doctrine. I could use false evidence to justify something that just happened to be true. You see, when you start with false evidence, you cannot make a judgment about the conclusion. The conclusion can be true or false. The only thing that we can conclude is that the evidence presented is useless for establishing the truth. Hence, if you are going to persuade others of the truth, the goal doesn't justify the means used to reach that goal. You must use truth to persuade others of the truth, just as the apostles did. *"For our exhortation did not come from error or uncleanness, nor was it in deceit. But as we have been approved by God to be entrusted with the gospel, even so we speak, not as pleasing men, but God who tests our hearts"* (I Thessalonians 2:3-4).

Ways that the lack of truth are hidden

Earlier, we pointed out the need to keep passages within their proper context. However, what happens when a person pulls a passage out-of-context to justify a point? It gives only the illusion that truth is being presented. Consider Jesus' temptation in the wilderness by the Devil. *"Then the devil took Him up into the holy city, set Him on the pinnacle of the temple, and said to Him, "If You are the Son of God, throw Yourself down. For it is written: 'He shall give His angels charge over you,' and, 'In their hands they shall bear you up, Lest you dash your foot against a stone.'" Jesus said to him, "It is written again, 'You shall not tempt the LORD your God.'""* (Matthew 4:5-7). Satan quoted God's Word to challenge Jesus to prove his deity. Jesus countered by showing that Satan's use of the Bible was in conflict with the greater context of the Bible. Satan's use of the Scriptures contradicted what God had said elsewhere in the Bible and, therefore, was not true.

In a similar vein, many false ideas are promoted by only citing evidence favorable to the position. For example, those advocating salvation by faith alone will cite the passages that mention the necessity of faith to be saved, but they neglect to refer to passages like Acts 2:38 which mention other things related to salvation. The Psalmist stated, *"The sum of Your word is truth"* (Psalm 119:160). Using only a portion of the Bible to give the impression of credence to a false idea is mishandling the Truth.

Many times falsehoods are justified by counting on the laziness of the audience. Few are like the noble-minded

Bereans who searched their Scriptures to verify the truth of the arguments (Acts 17:10-11). One way to slip in falsehood is to make two or more claims, but only justify a portion of the claims. There is a natural tendency to assume that if part of the points are true, then the remainder must also be true. There is a classic example of this in Jesus' sermon on the mount. *"You have heard that it was said, 'You shall love your neighbor and hate your enemy'"* (Matthew 5:43). Even to this day I have heard people say that the Old Testament taught hate while the New Testament teaches love. Yet, both the Old and New Testaments were written by the same God! How can there be such a contrast? The falsehood had become accepted by Jesus' day because it was hidden behind a truth. The law of Moses did teach that you should love your neighbor (Leviticus 19:18). But, it did not teach the Israelites to hate their enemies. Quite the opposite. In Leviticus 19:17, it was stated *"You shall not hate your brother in your heart."* Even foreigners were to be loved. *"The stranger who dwells among you shall be to you as one born among you, and you shall love him as yourself; for you were strangers in the land of Egypt: I am the LORD your God."* (Leviticus 19:34). How were enemies to be treated? *"If you meet your enemy's ox or his donkey going astray, you shall surely bring it back to him again. If you see the donkey of one who hates you lying under its burden, and you would refrain from helping it, you shall surely help him with it."* (Exodus 23:4-5). Or as Proverbs 25:21-22 clearly states, *"If your enemy is hungry, give him bread to eat; and if he is thirsty, give him water to* drink; for so you will heap coals of fire on his head, and the LORD will reward you."

A similar method is to give so much "proof" that your audience is overwhelmed. This is a favored technique used by the Jehovah's Witnesses. Their material is loaded with scriptural references – so loaded that few bother to look up the verses – but if you do you will often find that the verses cited have little or nothing to do with the arguments that they are presenting. The citations only give the appearance of evidence. Beware of the preacher who cites passages without actually turning to them and reading them. It is very easy to interject a falsehood when such is done.

Accepting what cannot be proven

When Jesus was proving his deity, he noted, *"If I bear witness of myself, my witness is not true"* (John 5:31). Jesus never told a falsehood (John 8:13-14), but he noted that arguing from insufficient evidence does not establish truth. Throughout the Bible there is a requirement for multiple witnesses to be used as the basis of judgment (Deuteronomy 17:6; 19:15; Matthew 18:16; II Corinthians 13:1-2; I Timothy 5:19). Yet, brethren will ignore this point if the statement is juicy enough to shock the hearer. What is stated might be true, but it could also be false. Even Jesus did not want us to believe on him by his word alone, so even if the most honest brother states he witnessed something, his witness alone does not establish the truth.

Sellers of various products will often use anecdotal evidence as proof that their product really works. The

greatest problem with anecdotal evidence is the fact that
some people get better even if nothing is done. Usually
there is no proof that person improved *because* he used
the product. In addition, many testimonials are not
verifiable. "Susan in Grand Island, Michigan, says, 'I took
X and my life has never been better!'" So how do you get
a hold of Susan to see if that is really what she said? You
see, the sellers of product X are certain that most of us will
never bother to check.

People who believe in modern-day miracles will rely
on the same anecdotal evidence. "I was feeling ill, so-
and-so prayed over me, and I got better." Was the
improvement *because* of the prayer or was it simply a
coincident?

And have you noticed how often third-hand evidence
is presented to "prove" that miracles are happening
today? I once asked a man if he had proof that miracles
were happening today. He told me that a friend of his
had seen a man drink a cup of coffee that he was told
had poison it because this man's wife was trying to get rid
of him, and he didn't suffer any ill effects! So how can this
story of a story be verified? I've known a few who tried. I
have a book written by a man who believes in miracles
who was trying to verify the stories. He had been
searching for five years at the time he wrote his book. He
hadn't been able to verify any story yet, but he knows they
must be out there – somewhere. I heard on the radio five
years after he wrote his book – he was still looking.
Another man told me of looking for evidence of miracles.
His friend told him that he had recently prayed for a man
in India to be healed of blindness and the prayer was

answered. The problem was this man did not know the man who was blind. He believed the man existed and was blind because someone told him that it was so. Similarly, he does not know that the man was healed of blindness. He was only told that the unknown blind man was now seeing. Do you see the many opportunities for fraud to be perpetuated? My response was to ask how much money was requested by the informer from India. Look again at the evidence of miracles presented in the Bible. If one person involved in the events wanted to commit a fraud, could it have been done? What you will quickly find is that it is impossible. There are too many independent people involved. Evidence that miracle took place was verified by multiple sources – many of whom had no reason to desire that a miracle take place. Consider as example, the evidence offered for the resurrection of Jesus. Paul tells us over 500 people witnessed the resurrection (I Corinthians 15:5-8). How many claims of miracles today offer sufficient, verifiable evidence?

Rejecting what isn't there

We all understand that a bad argument does not prove an idea to be true. It may be subtle, but just because a bad argument is made for an idea, it does not imply that the idea is false. A bad argument is just that – a bad argument! The idea under consideration must be proved or disproved by some other means. However, it is our natural tendency to reject all when a portion is wrong. For example, people involved in denominations write on the subject of money. Often their supporting evidence is clearly a misuse of the Scriptures. Does this mean that their ideas are bad? No, it just means that they don't know how to prove their point. It is still possible to go through the writings and glean the good ideas and the few good proofs.

Unfortunately, I have seen this faulty reasoning used against brethren. Because a man holds an incorrect view on one topic, people treat him as if everything he states is false. I'm sure much of this comes from laziness. It is easier to reject everything than to carefully examine every point. As an example, I know of a man who holds a false position concerning God's covenants. This man happened to run across evidence of fraud being perpetuated within the church in another country. Almost no one would even look at the evidence he had gathered because of his stand on an unrelated matter. As a result the fraud continued for many years. You see, his false belief did not imply he was dishonest.

People in arguments often fall back on this tendency to reject the whole when only a portion is disproved. Politicians will accuse their opponents of taking a controversial stand. They will then prove how that stand is wrong. There is only one thing missing – they never prove that their opponent holds the wrong position, they merely accuse him. The tactic is called straw-man arguments. You are not able to defeat the real person, so you create a dummy that is easily defeated and attack the dummy. In the ensuing fray, everyone forgets that the real opponent is not the dummy. Unfortunately, the use of straw-men arguments happens very frequently in religious debates. Those who stoop to such tactics need to realize that misrepresenting your opponent's position is a form of lying; you are lying to the audience about what your opponent believes. Now, I understand that a times it is difficult to present an opponents position accurately when you don't subscribe to it, but frequently I hear arguments where the person doesn't even come close.

A good example of straw-man arguments is found in how people fought against the spread of Christianity in the days of the apostles. *"For what if some did not believe? Will their unbelief make the faithfulness of God without effect? Certainly not! Indeed, let God be true but every man a liar. As it is written: "That You may be justified in Your words, And may overcome when You are judged." But if our unrighteousness demonstrates the righteousness of God, what shall we say? Is God unjust who inflicts wrath? (I speak as a man.) Certainly not! For then how will God judge the world? For if the truth of God has increased through my lie to His glory, why am I also still judged as a sinner? And why not say, "Let us do evil that good may come"? --as we are slanderously reported and as some affirm that we say. Their condemnation is just"* (Romans 3:3-8). This statement by Paul illustrates several of the points I have just made. Just because someone, who should have known better, is found unfaithful; his unfaithfulness does not change the truth about the faithfulness of God. If a man who is sinful teaches the truth, he will be justly punished for his sin; but his sinfulness is not a reason to reject the truth of God. In fact, Paul had to contend with people who falsely claimed that he stated "Let us do evil that good may come." That claim was a straw-man argument. It is easily shown to be false, but it was not a position that Paul held, though it was attributed to him.

Another example is found in Acts 17:5-8. *"But the Jews who were not persuaded, becoming envious, took some of the evil men from the marketplace, and gathering a mob, set all the city in an uproar and attacked the house of Jason, and sought to bring them out to the people. But when they did not find them, they dragged Jason and some brethren to the rulers of the city, crying out, "These who have turned the world upside down have come here too. 'Jason has harbored them, and these are all acting contrary to the decrees of Caesar, saying there is another king--Jesus.' And they troubled the crowd and the rulers of the city when they heard these things. "* Notice that in the middle of the Jews' accusation is the claim that the Christians were "all acting contrary to the decrees of Caesar." Such was a false accusation (Romans 13:1), but most people forget that an accusation is not proof.

Similar to a straw-man argument is an attack on an opponent's character. Instead of dealing with the issue at hand, the opponent is accused of having shady motives. When debating people over whether the Bible permits preachers to be located in one congregation, I have frequently been accused of simply trying to protect my job as a preacher. In other words, my opponents figure that the only reason I argue against them is because I make my living in a way that they oppose. The argument is not proof of what is true. It is merely a distraction technique designed to place doubt on the evidence that I have presented. It is no different than an atheist arguing, "Of course you would expect him to say God exists, he is a preacher!"

Paul once dealt with the opposite problem. He was accused of not being an apostle because he did not ask those he was teaching to support him (I Corinthians 9:1-15). We do not know exactly the argument used against Paul, but from his defense we can see that people were trying to spread doubt concerning his teaching because he did not behave as they thought he should. *"For I consider that I am not at all inferior to the most eminent apostles. Even though I am untrained in speech, yet I am not in knowledge. But we have been thoroughly manifested among you in all things. Did I commit sin in humbling myself that you might be exalted, because I preached the gospel of God to you free of charge? I robbed other churches, taking wages from them to minister to you. And when I was present with you, and in need, I was a burden to no one, for what I lacked the brethren who came from Macedonia supplied. And in everything I kept myself from being burdensome to you, and so I will keep myself. As the truth of Christ is in me, no one shall stop me from this boasting in the regions of Achaia. Why? Because I do not love you? God knows! But what I do, I will also continue to do, that I may cut off the opportunity from those who desire an opportunity to be regarded just as we are in the things of which they boast. For such are false apostles, deceitful workers, transforming themselves into apostles of Christ "*(2 Corinthians 11:5-13).

One falsehood does not justify another falsehood

We have a common saying that two wrongs don't make a right. Generally we apply this to the urge to get revenge. Just because someone does me evil, it is not justification for me to return evil in turn (Romans 12:19-21). This lack of reasoning is used to justify sinning. Because brother X smokes, brother Y sees nothing wrong if he takes a drink or two socially. Brother Z then feels justified to use drugs recreationally because it is no worse than what brother Y is doing. This is one reason sinful behavior easily spreads (I Corinthians 5:6). The good or bad behavior of another is not proof as to whether a certain action is right or wrong. Yet, people are often irrational.

Paul warned the Corinthians about giving a wrong impression. Idols are nothing, so food sacrificed to idols does not become corrupted because it use in the service to an idol. Yet some, seeing a brother eat meat that they know was used in idolatry might come to the wrong conclusion (I Corinthians 8:1-12). They might begin a practice that they did not fully believe to be righteous (Romans 14:19-23). Or they might wrongfully conclude that they could participate in idolatrous worship (I Corinthians 10:19-24).

The end does not justify the means

Commonly people conclude that if we arrive at truth, then the means used to arrive to that truth must be correct as well. Among the denominations people have decided that getting people to express a desire to follow Jesus is a good thing. This has lead to streamlining the conversion process so that they can get many people "saved" in a short period of time. Hence, we have street preachers telling people about Jesus and urging them to pray the sinner's prayer and then announcing that they are saved. If you ask for proof that such prayers actually save, often you are questioned as to how such a good thing can be wrong.

Paul had to deal with such arguments. There were people who thought that since God's grace will cover any sin that I might commit, I should sin big-time so that God's grace might be further demonstrated. Paul dealt with this false reasoning in Romans 5:20-6:23.

The idea that anything may be done so long as some good results is dangerously false. As Paul said in Romans 3:8, the claim is false. It is dangerous because too few people look beyond the result.

The Misuse of Truth

"Hold fast the pattern of sound words which you have heard from me, in faith and love which are in Christ Jesus" (II Timothy 1:13).

People are able to mishandle truths such that the truths create a falsehood.

Creating Falsehoods from Truth

We have spent an entire lesson on the importance of keeping the context of a passage in mind, but it will not hurt to further emphasize the point. In the sermon on the mount, Jesus talks of several traditional beliefs the Jews held, but which had no support in the Scriptures. In Matthew 5:38, Jesus talks about the idea of vengeance. *"You have heard that it was said, 'An eye for an eye and a tooth for a tooth.'"* Though Jesus attributes the saying to traditional beliefs, the quote is from the Old Testament. It is found in several places, such as Exodus 21:22-25, Leviticus 24:19-20, and Deuteronomy 19:16-21. If you read the context of each of these passages you will see that the phrase comes from instructions to judges. When a person was found guilty of certain crimes, the punishment measured out by the judge was to be based on the damage done by the person while committing the crime. However, we can see from Jesus' comments that the Jews had taken this concept and applied it to everyday life. No longer was it just used by an impartial judge to hand down appropriate punishment. Now the idea was that if I thought you did me wrong, I was justified in doing an equal amount of wrong back to you. The Jews had taken a statement that was true in one context and created a falsehood when applying it to a different context. They ended up contradicting God's law on personal vengeance. *"You shall not take vengeance, nor bear any grudge against the children of your people, but you shall love your neighbor as yourself: I am the LORD"* (Leviticus 19:18).

From the same sermon, we can see illustrated another way people create a falsehood from truth. In Matthew 5:21, Jesus again quotes from their traditional beliefs. *"You have heard that it was said to those of old, 'You shall not murder, and whoever murders will be in danger of the judgment.'"* The quote as a whole is not found in the Old Testament. Instead, it is a conjoining of two separate passages. *"You shall not murder"* is from the Ten Commandments, recorded in Exodus 20:13 and Deuteronomy 5:17. The second part, though, appears to be a loose summary of Numbers 35:29-31. *"And these things shall be a statute of judgment to you throughout your generations in all your dwellings. Whoever kills a person, the murderer shall be put to death on the testimony of witnesses; but one witness is not sufficient testimony against a person for the death penalty. Moreover you shall take no ransom for the life of a murderer who is guilty of death, but he shall surely be put to death."* Notice that the tradition Jesus quotes warns of the possibility of a trial if someone commits murder. The

Old Testament talks in much firmer terms. A murderer will be brought to trial. Even prior to the Old Law, God made a covenant with mankind in the days of Noah and stated, *"Surely for your lifeblood I will demand a reckoning; from the hand of every beast I will require it, and from the hand of man. From the hand of every man's brother I will require the life of man. Whoever sheds man's blood, By man his blood shall be shed; For in the image of God He made man."* (Genesis 9:5-6). By combining a truth with a sort-of-truth, the impact of God's law was watered down, giving the false impression that if you weren't careful, you might get caught if you murdered someone.

In all languages, words can take on a variety of meanings depending on the context in which they are used. For example, in English, the word "row" can mean a series of things, to propel by oars, or to make a lot of noise; which meaning applies depends on how the word is used. Hence, it is not surprising that error is created by applying the wrong definition of a word or phrase in a particular context. I once argued with a man who insisted "Christ's use of the word 'whosoever,' like that of God and Moses, referred only to the Jews of Israel - 'whosoever' in Old Testament Israel." He then used Leviticus 20:2, Exodus 31:15, and Leviticus 19:20-21 as proof that "whosoever" refers to the Jewish nation. Just because "whosoever" referred to a limited group in one context does not imply that it retains the same limited application in all contexts.

A similar mistaken argument is made with the Greek word "psallo" used in Ephesians 5:19 and generally translated as "making melody." Countless people have turned to dictionaries and read that the word means "to play a stringed instrument." The dictionaries are closed and they proclaim, "See, the Bible allows the use of musical instruments!" The problem is that was the meaning of psallo in classical Greek. If they had continued to read the dictionary, they would have learn that by the days in which the Septuagint translation was composed, the meaning of psallo had morphed into "to sing with a harp or to sing psalms." Then just a bit further you find that by the days of the New Testament the word had changed further to mean "to sing a hymn or sing praise." By applying the classical Greek meaning of a word to its New Testament usage, people have taken two truths to create an erroneous position.

Falsehoods created by taking Truth out of order

Just because one idea follows from another, it does not imply you may reverse the order. For example, this is a true statement: "If Jim was President of the United States, then he was over 35 years old." It is true because the Constitution of the United States requires Presidents to be over the age of 35. However, the following reversal is not true: "If Jim was over 35 years old, then he was President of the United States." A lot of people have passed the age of 35 without becoming President.

When a statement is expressed in the from of an "if" ... "then", the part between the "if" and the "then" is called the premise of the statement. The part that comes after the "then" is call the conclusion of the statement. Just because the premise of a statement leads to a certain conclusion, it does not imply that conclusion will lead to the premise.

A form of this unreasonable reasoning is when a person appeals to the consequence of an action to justify (or reject) the action. "Since good comes from X; therefore, X is true." Or, "since bad comes from X; therefore, X is false." The Salvation Army is a religion built on the idea that God expects Christians to aid the less fortunate, which is true. But they then proceed to accomplish that end by a variety of means. To members of this denomination, it doesn't matter how good is accomplished, so long as the end is reached. The liberal movement within the church has done much the same. In the 1950's it was argued that orphans needed caring. James 1:27 is proof that God views it as a Christian's duty. Hence, they concluded that any means may be used to reach that goal because the goal is good.

The extra difficulty in dealing with these types of issues is that a lot of emotion can be generated by keeping everyone's attention focused on the outcome. When emotions ride high, few are inclined to reason out whether God would be pleased.

Nadab and Abihu essentially reasoned in this manner. Incense need to be offered before God, so they wrongly concluded that it didn't matter how the offering was conducted, so long as the goal was reached. They harshly learned that God wants obedience in all that He commands (Leviticus 10:1-3). God told Moses and Aaron, "*By those who come near Me I must be regarded as holy; and before all the people I must be glorified.*"

When man decides how to accomplish God's will, it is man who is glorified and not God.

Falsehoods created by shifting quantities

A times facts are made to appear as related ideas by subtle shifts in the quantities involved. Perhaps it is best show with an illustration. "All whales are mammals. Some fish are not whales. Therefore, some fish are mammals." The conclusion is false because it was never proven that whales are fish. The two statements are actually independent facts, so they cannot be joined to create another truth.

These particular mis-reasonings are often difficult to spot because the shifting quantities. We went from "all whales" to "some fish." The added complication interferes with analyzing the statements.

Another example is found in the statement, "Everyone loves someone; therefore, there is someone whom everyone loves." The falsehood is created by assuming that only one person is being loved in the first portion of the statement. Everyone can love someone, but multiple objects of affection can be involved.

The same error is made in the use of Romans 5:12, "*Therefore, just as through one man sin entered the world, and death through sin, and thus death spread to all men, because all sinned.*" Many read this statement and assume that there is one sin of which everyone is considered guilty. The verse does not state there is only one type of sin involved, yet many assume that Adam's sin is inherited by his descendants. This is particularly amazing since Paul points out that everyone sins and then a few lines later states, "*Nevertheless death reigned from Adam to Moses, even over those who had not sinned according to the likeness of the transgression of Adam, who is a type of Him who was to come*" (Romans 5:14). Paul is talking about all sins and not a single sin which everyone inherits.

Faulty Comparisons

"For we are not bold to class or compare ourselves with some of those who commend themselves; but when they measure themselves by themselves and compare themselves with themselves, they are without understanding" (II Corinthians 10:12).

The Bandwagon

Most people find comfort in knowing that others feel the same about a position as they do. Yet, just because others agree, it does not indicate whether a particular position is true or false. Jesus warned, *"Enter by the narrow gate; for wide is the gate and broad is the way that leads to destruction, and there are many who go in by it. Because narrow is the gate and difficult is the way which leads to life, and there are few who find it"* (Matthew 7:13-14; see also Luke 13:23-24). From this we must conclude that a majority position is a better indicator of falsehood than of truth. The Proverb writer warns that even if others support you in error, the error will not go unpunished (Proverbs 11:21; 16:5).[3]

Do you remember trying to convince your mother to buy you a new lunch box because "Everyone has a new

---

[3]In several modern translations, such as the NASB'95 and the NIV, the literal Hebrew phrase "hand to hand" is translated as "assuredly" or "be sure of this." I am uncertain as to why the change was made.

one!"? Too often sin is justified by this same lack of thought. The world lies in the power of Satan, but we must not be of the world (I John 5:19). Just because "everyone" is participating in a sin, it does not mean the sin is acceptable. *"Therefore, since Christ suffered for us in the flesh, arm yourselves also with the same mind, for he who has suffered in the flesh has ceased from sin, that he no longer should live the rest of his time in the flesh for the lusts of men, but for the will of God. For we have spent enough of our past lifetime in doing the will of the Gentiles – when we walked in lewdness, lusts, drunkenness, revelries, drinking parties, and abominable idolatries. In regard to these, they think it strange that you do not run with them in the same flood of dissipation, speaking evil of you"* (1 Peter 4:1-4). Your friends in the world may not understand, but you must!

Roman Catholicism is the largest denomination in the world, yet does it size make its teachings correct? I have had members of this denomination point out its size in the middle of a disagreement as if to say "all these people can't be wrong." But is this any different than brethren who take comfort in the fact that they are a part of the "mainstream" churches? "Mainstream" just means the majority follow a particular set of beliefs. The fact that a majority believes a particular doctrine does prove the doctrine.

Guilt by Association

Some will reject a truth because it was delivered by the wrong source. Sometimes it is referred to as "killing the messenger." In Luke 11:14-15, Jesus healed a mute man by casting out a demon. The work was obviously good, but those who opposed Jesus could not accept it, so they accused Jesus of having power over demons because Satan granted him that power. The remainder of Luke 11 shows Jesus making the Pharisees look very foolish, which did not endear Jesus to them. As a result, *"And as He said these things to them, the scribes and the Pharisees began to assail Him vehemently, and to cross-examine Him about many things, lying in wait for Him, and seeking to catch Him in something He might say, that they might accuse Him"* (Luke 11:53-54). It did not matter that Jesus spoke the truth about the Pharisees and their beliefs. All that mattered to them was finding evidence that Jesus was wrong in some fashion. If they could prove that, then they would feel justified in rejecting all that the Christ had said.

The same thing happened to the blind man in John 9:24-34. When Jesus was accused of being a sinner, the man ably pointed out that sinners ought not to be able to heal. When he further turned the Pharisees accusations on themselves, the Pharisees declared that he was a sinner because he was born blind (John 9:34). This was sufficient justification to throw the man out of the synagogue. By accusing the man of sin, they felt justified in ignoring all that he said, right or wrong.

A similar charge was brought against Paul, *"'For his letters,' they say, 'are weighty and powerful, but his bodily presence is weak, and his speech contemptible'"* (II Corinthians 10:10). Some felt justified in ignoring Paul's commands because he was not an impressive man in person. Paul warned that his teaching remained true, whether it was delivered by letter or in person (II Corinthians 10:11).

Justification by Association

This line of argumentation is often used to endorse products. "Because X says it is good, it must be very good." It can also be used to support a position. "X believes this way, so, it must be true." In the Corinthian church, people were creating artificial divisions and then giving these divisive positions the appearance of credence by claiming that a well-known leader held the position. *"Now I plead with you, brethren, by the name of our Lord Jesus Christ, that you all speak the same thing, and that there be no divisions among you, but that you be perfectly joined together in the same mind and in the same judgment. For it has been declared to me concerning you, my brethren, by those of Chloe's household, that there are contentions among you. Now I say this, that each of you says, "I am of Paul," or "I am of Apollos," or "I am of Cephas," or "I am of Christ." Is Christ divided? Was Paul crucified for you? Or were you baptized in the name of Paul?"* (1 Corinthians 1:10-13; see also I Corinthians 3:1-8).

The fault is that who believes a certain position does not make the position true or false. If it is a false position, it just means that some famous people have been snookered into believing it. If it is a true position it just means that on this particular point the famous person happens to believe the truth. But truth doesn't become more real because of who believes it. Truth stands on its own. So does it matter if Oprah Winfrey says Jesus would not condemn homosexuality? Is it relevant that Billy Graham says baptism is not necessary for salvation?

Take note that sometimes the famous person called in for endorsement is not an expert in the matter being endorsed. Just how learned is Oprah Winfrey on Jesus' doctrine anyway?

But even when a knowledgeable person takes a particular position, the fact that an "authority" holds a particular view doesn't make the view true. Every authority on any subject holds his or her own particular biases. When using a commentary, it is important to know the religious background of the commentator. For example, Albert Barnes was a Presbyterian. Since Presbyterians are followers of the teachings of John Calvin, you would not expect to find much in Barnes' writings contradicting the Calvinist point-of-view. Adam Clarke was a Methodist, so you would expect Clarke's commentary to have a bias supporting the Methodist view of Christianity. A. T. Robertson was a Baptist, so you would expect to find him justifying Baptist doctrine. Instead, quotes from commentaries become more notable when the commentator makes note of views which contradict their denomination's stand. It is interesting when a commentator must admit that his brand of religion is wrong on a particular point. The fact that a commentator supports his own denomination's belief is not noteworthy. Commentaries and other reference material do not establish truth.

Arguing Incompetence

It is easy to fall into the trap of thinking that your opponent only holds his position because of his ignorance. After all, he disagrees with you, so how much can he know?

Debaters will sometimes point out that their opponent hasn't gone to a theological seminary, or isn't fluent in Greek or Hebrew, and therefore, is somehow unqualified to discuss the matters at hand. Even when the point is shown to be worthless, it still leaves doubt in the audience's mind. At times the doubt is injected with the simple charge, "You haven't thought this through very well, have you." Or, they may claim that your argument is not worth answering. The real problem is that you are "wrong" before your response is even considered.

Sometimes the ridicule becomes particularly harsh. "You would have to be an idiot to believe such a thing!" Or, "That group is nothing more than a cult!" Or, "If you are going to believe that, I'm not talking to you anymore." None of these statements answer the opponent's position. Instead, they ridicule the person and apply pressure to separate oneself from the frowned upon view.

Another form of this line of argument is to claim that only the church or certain church leaders can correctly interpret Scripture. Therefore, any stand contrary to the church must be false. The Scriptures teach, though, that they are truth (John 17:17). While the church is required to support the truth (I Timothy 3:15), the Bible does not teach that decisions of the church are always true. If we need evidence of that, we need only go to the seven churches of Asia in Revelation 2 and 3 to see that churches do not always follow the Lord properly.

There is no easy defense against such charges. To defend yourself will distract you from the points that need to be made. At worse, you will come across as being prideful. The best you can do is to ignore the charge and do a thorough job of laying out the evidence. If I am expecting such a response, I will hold back part of my proof when making my points. When my competency is challenged, I then proceed to layout so much evidence that the one making the charge suddenly looks foolish because he doesn't have any supporting material.

Arguing from Illustrations

Illustrations are a fine way of getting a point across. Some ideas are difficult to grasp, so comparing the difficult idea to a simple, everyday event eases the learning. Often the illustrations also make the story more memorial. Jesus defined "neighbor" by telling the story of good Samaritan (Luke 10:25-37). The point was well told that even those unfamiliar with the Bible know of the story and its moral.

A problem, though, arises when illustration is offered as proof. An illustration clarifies, but it rarely proves a point. For example, picking on the People for the Ethical Treatment of Animals (PETA) again, PETA once drew an analogy between the holocaust and the treatment of animals in scientific studies. While the analogy illustrates how severe PETA considers experiments with animals, the illustration doesn't prove it is wrong. The holocaust was infamous for how poorly humans were mistreated. Yet, the illustration does not prove that animals are equivalent to humans. PETA may think they are, but the illustration doesn't prove this point, it only illustrates what PETA believes.

In a sense, arguing from illustrations is similar to straw-man arguments. A connection is drawn between to points and then arguments are made against one set of points. People naturally think that the argument against one set of points then applies to the other set. They rarely stop to wonder if the connection was truly legitimate or not.

In Colossians 2:10-15, Paul compares circumcision and baptism to show the salvation we have in Christ. Some have argued that since babies are circumcised, they can then be baptized as infants. The problem is that the analogy between circumcision and baptism was overworked to draw more than what was being illustrated. There are limits to the parallel of circumcision and baptism. After all, only boys are circumcised, so should we say that only boys should be baptized?

Another illustration is found in the argument that Christians are God's children (Romans 8:16). When a child displeases his father in an earthly family, he may be scolded, but he is still a part of the family. Hence, it is argued that when a Christian displeases God by sinning, he still remains God's child and will always be saved. Notice how one simple illustration is stretched to greater and greater applications. Yet, I know of families where a wayward son was disinherited. The parents still loved the child, but they couldn't support his sinful life. Though the argument can be defeated within the illustration, it still does not excuse the misuse of the illustration to mean more than for what the original author used it.

Diversion

Diversion is the attempt to connect an unrelated idea to the topic currently being discussed. Though the new topic is a separate issue, the person you are talking to will insist that the new topic be addressed first before going back to the original topic. The unstated goal is that you will never get back to the original topic.

When a position is difficult to defend, people will commonly shift the emphasis of their arguments to another, easier to defend, position. For example, when arguing that abortion or euthanasia is right, the defenders claim it must be right because individual has the right to choose. But the right to choose is a choice between two right actions. You have the right to choose to buy a new car or put the money in the bank; either action is legal. But a person's right to choose does not make abortion or euthanasia right or wrong. First abortion or euthanasia must be proven to be ethical, then we can talk about your right to chose.

Diversion is also used as a distraction technique. When talking with some about why they are not attending services, they begin to talk about the hypocrites in the church. The fact that hypocrites exist doesn't prove whether a person should be at church; it is not as if hypocrisy is a communicable disease. In fact, I wonder who is the bigger hypocrite, the one attending but failing in living the Christian life, or the one who thinks he is a Christian but refuses to attend.

Lumping Too Much Together

Just because two ideas lead to the same conclusion, it does not mean the two ideas are related. For example, "All teenagers have two legs. All ostriches have two legs. Therefore, all teenagers are ostriches."

Similarly, just because one or more events came to a particular conclusion doesn't mean it will always have the same result. Just because the Huskers won two years in a row, it doesn't mean they have a good chance of winning the third year. There are many factors involved. As an example, it is sometimes argued that if women are allowed to sit in on business meetings, the next thing you know they will be leading prayers or preaching. The presence of women in business meetings does not necessarily imply that women will exceed their authority in the church. Where it has happened has been due to other factors, such as a misunderstanding of authority or a strong influence of feminism in the church. The improper concluding state does not imply that every preceding event was the cause. To argue whether women should be present in a congregation's business meeting must be addressed on its own merits. (For clarity, if a particular state necessarily follows from a preceding one, it is worthy to consider in an argument.)

Just because a part has a property does not mean the whole has the same property. One could possibly argue, "The body is composed of invisible atoms; therefore, the body is invisible." A part can have different characteristics from the whole of which it is a part. You can see this faulty reasoning in the argument that since a church is made up of individuals, anything the individual can do, the church can do. As an individual, I can operate a business, does this mean that congregations can raise funds by operating a business? Many denominations have decided the answer is "yes." They operate book stores, day care facilities, apartment renting, and many other activities for profit. However, in I Timothy 5:1-16 we can see that there are some activities which are not a church's responsibility, but are an individual Christian's responsibility. Especially notice verse 16, *"If any believing man or woman has widows, let them relieve them, and do not let the church be burdened, that it may relieve those who are really widows."*

The opposite is also a problem. Just because the whole has a certain property, it doesn't mean that the parts share the same property. This line of poor reasoning is commonly known as the division fallacy. A person could argue, "The church may come together to partake of the Lord's Supper; therefore, the Lord's Supper may be taken by individuals apart from the church."

Gambler's Fallacy

If you randomly flip a coin and three times in a row it comes up "heads," what are the odds that the next flip of the coin will also come up heads? Many people will naturally assign very low odds to such occurring. It is true that if you set out to flip a coin for the purpose of getting four heads in a row, the odds of succeeding are very low (½ to the fourth power or 6.25%). However, the original question was tricky. Three of those flips have already came up heads. At this moment in time, what is the odds of getting another head. The true answer is 50%; the same probability of flipping a heads on the first toss.

Random events are just that, they are random. Prior events do not effect their behavior. Yet we have a hard time dismissing our prior knowledge when dealing with a current event. This is the trap gamblers fall into. They pore money into slot machines because they "know" that they can't lose every time. In fact, if they have lost on a particular machine a large number of times in a row, then they feel that a win must be due shortly. The reality is that unless a machine is rigged, the odds of winning remain slim each an every time the handle is pulled. The past does not influence future probabilities.

Human beings are very good at spotting patterns. But we must be careful not to assign patterns to things that occur randomly. Have you ever heard of the old saying, "bad things occur in threes?" Do they really come in sets of three or do you notice the third bad event more after two bad things happened?

We also do this in talking about our runs of luck. "My good luck just ran out." Or, "I better stay at home today, I'm having a run of bad luck." If it is truly "luck" then we are discussing random events. There are no runs.

Some things do just occur randomly. *"I returned and saw under the sun that – the race is not to the swift, nor the battle to the strong, nor bread to the wise, nor riches to men of understanding, nor favor to men of skill; but time and chance happen to them all"* (Ecclesiastes 9:11). We tend to think that everything must have a cause. But it is not necessarily so. Jesus once pointed this flaw in reasoning out to his audience. *"There were present at* that season some who told Him about the Galileans whose blood Pilate had mingled with their sacrifices. And Jesus answered and said to them, "Do you suppose that these Galileans were worse sinners than all other Galileans, because they suffered such things? "I tell you, no; but unless you repent you will all likewise perish. "Or those eighteen on whom the tower in Siloam fell and killed them, do you think that they were worse sinners than all other men who dwelt in Jerusalem? "I tell you, no; but unless you repent you will all likewise perish" (Luke 13:1-5). We must be careful to distinguish between things that randomly occur and things that are within our control.

Time Associations

Because two things happen together, we assume one caused the other. One could argue, "As a child's shoe size increases, his handwriting improves; therefore, people with big feet have better handwriting." Many arguments for modern-day miracles are of this form of illogical reasoning. Because X prayed for Y to get better and Y improved; therefore, X has the gift of healing. The prayer and the healing are two events. It is possible that the two are related, but it is just as probable that the two just happen to occur in the same time frame. The closeness of when they occurred is not sufficient evidence that they are related events.

Because one thing happens shortly after another we assume the first is the cause. So one could argue, "Roosters crow just before the sun rises; therefore, rooster crowing causes the sun to rise." Here the events are tied, but we did not perceive the correct tie. Rosters crow because dawn precedes the rising sun. Yet often once we latch onto a particular conclusion, we cannot be persuaded that our assumed pattern of cause and effect could be wrong.

This type of incorrect associations has caused many people to come to the wrong conclusion concerning the conversion of Cornelius, recorded in Acts 10. Because Cornelius and his household were baptized in the Holy Spirit prior to their baptism in water, people have concluded that Cornelius and his household were saved before baptism. Cornelius's two baptisms did occur closely in time, but if the baptism in the Spirit saved Cornelius, then why did Peter order Cornelius baptized in water? What is overlooked is that Cornelius' baptism in the Spirit was evidence that God has accepted Gentiles as candidates to be His children – something that had not be apparent before to Christians. The baptism in the Spirit was evidence that these Gentiles could become Christians with God's blessing; but it does not necessarily give evidence that they were saved prior to their obedience to God's command (I Peter 3:21).

Regression

Most things return to an average or normal state. For example, many ill people will eventually get well even without treatment. Those in the medical profession understand this, so treatments are carefully studied to rule out normal healing versus an improvement due to the treatment.

However, this same natural event is exploited by quacks. They can offer a "cure" that has nothing to do with the illness, knowing that some will get better anyway. Since people seek out treatment at the extreme of their illness, they assume the cure given was the cause that returned them to normality. Those who don't return to normality die; therefore, removing any negative publicity.

Once again, we must determine if a claim of healing power was an actual effect or if the person recovered normally. Miracles in the Bible were notable in that there was no recovery period – something that doesn't happen in a normal recovery.

Going Overboard

"The word of the LORD came to me again, saying, 'What do you mean when you use this proverb concerning the land of Israel, saying: 'The fathers have eaten sour grapes, And the children's teeth are set on edge'? As I live,' says the Lord GOD, 'you shall no longer use this proverb in Israel'" (Ezekiel 18:1-3).

Over Generalization

We all assume the sun will rise tomorrow even though we know there will come a day when it will no longer exist (II Peter 3:10). We make these generalizations because it allows for simpler plans and thoughts. If we tried covering every possibility, no matter how remote in every plan, we would get so bogged down the plans would never be executed. Humans need to generalize, but there is a danger of forgetting that generalizations are not precise. We might say that "Birds can fly," but this doesn't mean that penguins, ostriches, and the extinct dodos are not birds. This is why James warned about the making of future plans. *"Come now, you who say, "Today or tomorrow we will go to such and such a city, spend a year there, buy and sell, and make a profit"; whereas you do not know what will happen tomorrow. For what is your life? It is even a vapor that appears for a little time and then vanishes away. Instead you ought to say, "If the Lord wills, we shall live and do this or that." But now you boast in your arrogance. All such boasting is evil"* (James 4:13-

16). We need to make future plans, but we must always keep in mind that the future is not within our control. When we begin to think that our generalizations are fixed, then we fall into the trap of pride.

There are many ways we tend to rely too heavily on generalizations. If something happens once, we quite naturally assume that it will happen again. Mrs. Smith took brand-X and improved; therefore, everyone who takes brand-X will see benefits. The problem is that we do not know if the taking of brand-X was a direct contributor to Mrs. Smith's improvement or simply an incidental fact. A lot of snake-oil is sold because of this. Belief in modern-day miracles is also perpetuated by unreasonable generalizations from very little information.

Even when you use a sample, you cannot be certain about the whole. Have you not noticed that polls usually will express their margin of error? Using a sample to conclude an absolute about the whole is an error in over generalization. Sampling is expressed in degrees of confidence, not absolutes. In a debate that I watched, one man stated "Baptism is not mentioned as a condition of salvation in John, the justification sections of Romans or Galatians, therefore baptism is not essential for salvation." There are several flaws in this argument, but notice that used a limited selection of the New Testament to make a conclusion about the entire New Testament. His argument purposely ignores the clear statement in I Peter 3:21, but notice that he couldn't take all of Romans because Romans 6 contradicts his position. He didn't want all of Galatians because Galatians 3:26 contradicts his position. The funny thing is, even with his narrow selection, he still missed his target. In John 3:5 Jesus said, *"unless one is born of water and the Spirit, he cannot enter the kingdom of God."* And only a few verses later we find that Jesus was making disciples via baptism (John 3:22, 26; 4:1). Now perhaps this man thought that you could be a disciple of Jesus without being saved, but I am not so persuaded.

Sometimes over generalizations appear in very subtle forms. Take the argument: "All dogs are animals. No cats are dogs. Therefore, no cats are animals." The flaw in the argument is that we were not shown that only dogs are animals. Dogs were overgeneralized to apply to all animals. The same flaw is seen in the argument: "All dogs are animals. Some pets are dogs. Therefore, some pets are not animals." The only way this statement could be true is if all animals were dogs.

Over generalizations can also occur when we make a text say too much. For example, what if I used II Timothy 4:2 which says *"Preach the word! Be ready in season and out of season. Convince, rebuke, exhort, with all longsuffering and teaching."* Hmm, preaching is to consist of convincing, rebuking, and exhortation; therefore, preaching should be 2/3 negative (convince and rebuke) and 1/3 positive (exhort). Paul's list was not meant to be used to determine proportions of time. Yet, I have seen people take the parable of the sower in Matthew 13 and argue that only 25% of the people you teach are going to remain faithful Christians.

We have mentioned straw men arguments in a previous lesson. Straw men arguments are built by assigning an extreme all-or-nothing position to your

opponent's arguments or beliefs and then arguing against
the extreme position instead of the opponent's actual
statements. After giving evidence that the Old Testament,
including the Ten Commandments, were no longer in
effect, I was given this counter argument, "He says the
Ten Commandments are no longer in effect, so he is
saying that you can lying, steal, and cheat on your
spouse." Generally, straw men arguments are built on
partial quotes or mis-representative quotes taken out of
context which are then over-generalized in application to
a particular problem. The removal of one covenant so
that another might take its place does not necessarily
mean that what constitutes sin has changed. For example,
lying was wrong under the old covenant because God
said in the Ten Commandments *"You shall not bear false
witness against your neighbor"* (Deuteronomy 5:20).
Lying is also wrong under the new covenant because Paul
tells us, *"Therefore, putting away lying, "Let each one of
you speak truth with his neighbor," for we are members of
one another"* (Ephesians 4:25).

We can also overreach a conclusion by arguing that a
conclusion must be false because the premise is false. All
you have really done is prove that you cannot use this
premise to reach the conclusion. For example, "If we
hang the criminal, he will die. Therefore, if we don't hang
the criminal, he will not die." The problem is that arguer is
ignoring the fact that a criminal can die by means other
than hanging. This particular mistake is often used when
arguing Mark 16:16 where Jesus said, *"He who believes
and is baptized will be saved; but he who does not
believe will be condemned."* We know that both belief

and baptism is needed for salvation. The second half of
Jesus' statement proves that faith is a necessary condition
for salvation. Some groups, such as the Baptists, have
long argued that because Jesus did not mention not
being baptized that baptism is, therefore, unnecessary to
salvation. Christians have countered saying that the
"and" in the statement proves that it is necessary. The
reality is that Mark 16:16 *by itself* is insufficient to prove
whether or not baptism is necessary. A lack of baptism
negates the premise which means the conclusion can be
true or false – a person could be saved or not saved. The
only way to determine whether baptism is necessary is
look at other statements, such as Acts 22:16 and I Peter
3:21, which show that baptism is a necessary condition
for salvation.

Oversimplification

We live in a complex world, so we simplify complex
thoughts to be better able to deal with them. However,
when a person simplifies an idea, he runs the risk of
reducing the idea down to the point of causing a
misrepresentation. The nature of God is incredibly
complex, yet some latch onto the idea that God is love (I
John 4:16) and conclude that there could not possibly be
a hell because a loving God would not send anyone to
eternal punishment.

The problem is that a few passages are used as if they
represent everything discussed on a particular topic.
Many denominations declare that salvation is by faith only
and cite John 3:16 as evidence. They will further declare
that it cannot be of works and cite Ephesians 2:8-9. But

the fact is that they are guilty of oversimplification. Salvation is mentioned in many more verses than these. The works mentioned in Ephesians 2:8-9 would not include baptism because Paul said, *"For we are His workmanship, created in Christ Jesus for good works, which God prepared beforehand that we should walk in them"* (Ephesians 2:10). Just prior, Paul stated, *"But God, who is rich in mercy, because of His great love with which He loved us, even when we were dead in trespasses, made us alive together with Christ (by grace you have been saved), and raised us up together, and made us sit together in the heavenly places in Christ Jesus"* (Ephesians 2:4-6). Notice that we were dead, but were made alive and raised up with Jesus. How was that accomplished? Paul tells us plainly in Romans 6:3-7 that this was done in baptism. It is also clearly seen in Colossians 2:12-13, *"buried with Him in baptism, in which you also were raised with Him through faith in the working of God, who raised Him from the dead. And you, being dead in your trespasses and the uncircumcision of your flesh, He has made alive together with Him, having forgiven you all trespasses."* The same ideas, death, being made alive, and being raised are presented, but are connected with baptism which is called a work of God – the very thing Paul said we were created for in Ephesians 2:10).

In the same way, a person can error by making judgments based on surface appearances instead of consider the whole. Jesus healed a man on the Sabbath day, which caused many Jews to be upset. But Jesus points out that they were looking at the issue only superficially. *"Moses therefore gave you circumcision (not that it is from Moses, but from the fathers), and you circumcise a man on the Sabbath. If a man receives circumcision on the Sabbath, so that the law of Moses should not be broken, are you angry with Me because I made a man completely well on the Sabbath? Do not judge according to appearance, but judge with righteous judgment"* (John 7:22-24). The Jews had oversimplified God's law and it was seen when one law was pitted against another. God doesn't issue conflicting laws (I Corinthians 14:33).

People also are guilty of superficial judgments when they determine how they will treat a person by his appearance. *"My brethren, do not hold the faith of our Lord Jesus Christ, the Lord of glory, with partiality. For if there should come into your assembly a man with gold rings, in fine apparel, and there should also come in a poor man in filthy clothes, and you pay attention to the one wearing the fine clothes and say to him, "You sit here in a good place," and say to the poor man, "You stand there," or, "Sit here at my footstool," have you not shown partiality among yourselves, and become judges with evil thoughts? Listen, my beloved brethren: Has God not chosen the poor of this world to be rich in faith and heirs of the kingdom which He promised to those who love Him? But you have dishonored the poor man. Do not the rich oppress you and drag you into the courts? Do they not blaspheme that noble name by which you are called?"* (James 2:1-7).

Another way that errors are made by oversimplification is by taking one definition of a word and applying it to all usages, even though the word may have multiple definitions. People have taken the Hebrew and Greek words for "wine" and stated that they always refer to alcoholic drinks. It is true that in some usages it these words are clearly referring to liquor of some sort, but it is not difficult to show that in many context the liquid in question cannot be alcoholic. For instance, in some passages it mentions the wine within the grapes or squeezing the wine from the grapes. Therefore, the words translated as wine have a broader range of meaning than it might first appear. It would be a mistake to assume every mention of "wine" is a reference to an alcoholic beverage.

We can also oversimplify by creating fake precision. A fake precision is created when we differentiate things that are essentially the same by harping on insignificant differences. As an example, in Matthew 5:22 Jesus warns against calling someone "raca" or a "fool." I have read detailed debates concerning the difference in meaning between these words. Yet, the reality is that in the original language, "raca" is the word for fool in Aramaic and "moros," which is translated "fool," is the Greek word for fool. It is absurd to argue the difference between a Aramaic fool and a Greek fool. In doing so causes a person to miss Jesus' point that it doesn't matter what language you use to insult someone, it remains wrong.

Similarly false doctrine is sometimes promoted by dividing synonyms to create the allusion of separate topics. For example, I have debated some who insist that salvation, justification, forgiveness, and sanctification are separate, independent topics. Therefore, if you point out

James 2:24 to show that you cannot be saved by faith alone, they will point out that the verse says "justified" and not "saved" – as if that made some sort of difference.

Questions
1) What error is made when a person oversimplifies the idea that God controls the world?
2) What error is made when a person oversimplifies the idea that God is all knowing?

Exclusions and Hypothetical Arguments

"The same day the Sadducees, who say there is no resurrection, came to Him and asked Him, saying: 'Teacher, Moses said that if a man dies, having no children, his brother shall marry his wife and raise up offspring for his brother. Now there were with us seven brothers. The first died after he had married, and having no offspring, left his wife to his brother. Likewise the second also, and the third, even to the seventh. Last of all the woman died also. Therefore, in the resurrection, whose wife of the seven will she be? For they all had her'" (Matthew 22:23-28).

Arguing by Exclusion

False doctrine often slips in under the guise of exclusion. A person will prove that a particular action is required from the Scriptures, but then concludes that it is only this way. For example, advocates of salvation by faith alone will cite verse after verse where faith is a requirement for salvation and then in their summary state, "You see, salvation is by faith alone." The problem is that they have not proved their point. To prove something exclusively exists, you must show one of two things: 1) a direct statement of exclusiveness, or 2) a complete lack of any other means of obtaining the desired goal. In the case of faith alone, the first does not exist. There is no statement in the Bible that states salvation comes by faith exclusively. That faith is required for salvation is easily proven, but the exclusion of any other requirements is not. In fact, there is only one first that discuss faith in the exclusive sense and that is James 2:24, which contradicts the faith alone position.

The psalmist stated, *"The entirety of Your word is truth"* (Psalm 119:160). Truth is found by considering the whole of what God said. When you only consider a portion, you can arrive at the wrong conclusion. When making a claim of exclusion and lacking a direct statement proving your point, you must examine every verse concerning the topic and show that it only happened in that manner. Since there is no statement stating that salvation is by faith alone, the supporter must show that every instance of salvation came only by faith. If you think about it, this is a tall order. There are a large number of passages dealing with salvation. The one in opposition is in a better position. To prove the supporter wrong, he needs only show one verse where there was requirement of something in addition to faith in order to obtain salvation. Passages such as Acts 2:38 and Acts 22:16 easily establish that faith is not the only requirement for salvation, therefore salvation is not by faith alone.

We must remember this when presenting the gospel to others. Arguments of exclusiveness are difficult to prove and easily defeated. When dealing with someone unfamiliar with the Bible, you are asking a lot for them to except an "only" position based on one or two verses. For example, we understand that the New Testament authorizes singing in worship and that instrumental music is excluded. Ephesians 5:19 and Colossians 3:16 show that singing is required, but they do not show that it is exclusively singing. That argument can only be proven by examining every place where music is mentioned in the New Testament and showing that it was only done with vocal music. This not as difficult as it might sound. There are only a few places where music is discussed in the New Testament. However, it is necessary to show these verses to properly prove the point. It is improper to ask others to accept arguments that we find unacceptable when applied to other topics.

A more subtle exclusive argument is to state that the truth must be one of two choices, then proving one choice isn't true so concluding it must be the other. This method of proof only works if the two choices do not overlap and if the two choice are the only two possible choices. For example, I could state "Either it is Tuesday or it is raining. It is not Tuesday, so it must be raining." The argument fails because it can be Tuesday and raining and it can be another day of the week and not be raining.

The Pharisees of Jesus' day frequently attempted to trap Jesus between two seemingly conflicting positions. *"Teacher, we know that You say and teach rightly, and You do not show personal favoritism, but teach the way of God in truth: Is it lawful for us to pay taxes to Caesar or not?"* (Luke 20:21-22). If Jesus stated that taxes should not be paid, they would turn him over to the governing authorities for rebellious statements. If Jesus stated that taxes should be paid, the Jews would turn on him because the Romans were an unpopular occupying force in their country. Jesus' answer showed that there was overlap in the two positions. *"'Show Me a denarius. Whose image and inscription does it have?' They answered and said, 'Caesar's.' And He said to them, 'Render therefore to Caesar the things that are Caesar's, and to God the things that are God's'"* (Luke 20:24-25). The Jews accepted and used Roman coinage in their daily transactions. Those coins were back by the power of the Roman government. It was inconsistent to both deny the government and benefit from the government at the same time.

Another example is found in John 8:3-5. *"Then the scribes and Pharisees brought to Him a woman caught in adultery. And when they had set her in the midst, they said to Him, "Teacher, this woman was caught in adultery, in the very act. Now Moses, in the law, commanded us that such should be stoned. But what do You say?'"* The law of Moses did command that adultery be punished by stoning (Deuteronomy 22:22). However, the Roman government at that time stated that only a Roman official could impose a death penalty. If Jesus indicated support for God's law, he would be in violation of man's law. However, Jesus pointed out a third position. These men had broken Moses' law. Read Deuteronomy 22:22 carefully and you will find that both the man and the woman were to be stoned, yet the Pharisees only brought the woman, though they claim they caught her in the act of adultery. Where was the man? This is why Jesus' simple statement, *"He who is without sin among you, let him throw a stone at her first"* (John 8:7), had such a devastating effect on the accusers. They knew they were wrong by accusing the woman while allowing the man freedom.

We must be careful not to make similar faulty arguments. For example, I could claim, "We can't both be right. You're wrong. Therefore, I'm right." The style of argument is called "black or white arguments." What is being ignored is the possibility that we both could be wrong. Most black or white arguments break down when it is shown that more than the two possibilities exist.

Several times we have shown the danger in arguing from the conclusion of an "if-then" statement. One point might be the natural consequence of another point, but to then assume that because the conclusion is true, the premise must be true is a falsehood. I could argue, "If it is raining, then the streets are wet. The streets are wet; therefore, it is raining." The fault lies in the fact that streets can be wet for more reason than that it is currently raining. Just because one thing leads to another does not imply that it is the only thing that leads to the conclusion.

Arguing from possibilities

Some become bent out of shape when you prove their favorite belief is not correct – especially if it is an action in which they have been involved. The argument thrown back is that it could have happened that way and if you deny it, then you are limiting the power of God. I have been told at one time or another, each of the following:

- Jesus could save by faith alone, so to deny it means you are limiting God's power.

- God is able to perform miracles if He so desired, so if you deny that they are occurring, you are trying to limit the power of God.
- God could have used evolution to create the world, so to argue against it is to limit how God works.

Taken at face value, the argument is worthless. No matter how I might present a case, I cannot limit God. *"For it is written: 'I will destroy the wisdom of the wise, And bring to nothing the understanding of the prudent.' Where is the wise? Where is the scribe? Where is the disputer of this age? Has not God made foolish the wisdom of this world?"* (I Corinthians 1:19-20). The reality is not whether some man has placed a limit on the power of God, what we must recognize is what God has stated He has done and will do. The point is not whether God could have saved men by faith alone, the question has God done so? (And the clear answer is "no" – James 2:24). It is not a question of whether God could do miracles today, it is whether we will acknowledge that God said the miracles would cease (I Corinthians 13:8-10).

Which of you would like to be tried for a murder and have the opposing lawyer argue that you could have pulled the trigger; therefore, it doesn't matter whether you actually did so or not. I could argue that yesterday it could have rained. Whether the possibility existed or not, the truth is that it did or did not rain. Possibilities do not establish the truth.

While God is infinite in power, He has told us that there are things He cannot do. God cannot sin (I John

1:5). God's promises cannot change (Hebrews 6:17-18). He cannot lie (Titus 1:2). He cannot deny Himself (II Timothy 2:13). Perhaps some would claim these are limits on the power of God. Yet, these are fundamental characteristics of God. If God could do these things, then He would not be the Almighty God that we worship.

Questions

1) Look at Deuteronomy 17:6. Why did Jesus let the adulterous woman in John 8 go, even though he knew she had sinned?
2) What other things can you think of that God cannot do?

Reviling What They Do Not Understand

"But there were also false prophets among the people, even as there will be false teachers among you, who will secretly bring in destructive heresies, even denying the Lord who bought them, and bring on themselves swift destruction. And many will follow their destructive ways, because of whom the way of truth will be blasphemed. ... But these, like natural brute beasts made to be caught and destroyed, speak evil of the things they do not understand, and will utterly perish in their own corruption" (II Peter 2:1-2, 12).

Reviling What They Do Not Understand - An appeal to ignorance

For some people, if they are unable to understand something, then it must be wrong. In discussing false teachers, Jude warns, *"But these speak evil of whatever they do not know; and whatever they know naturally, like brute beasts, in these things they corrupt themselves."* (Jude 10). It is easy to degrade what you do not understand. Because of fear of the unknown, people find it easier to accept such rejections. This one reason racism is difficult to overcome – people fear what they do not understand and it is easier to remain in fear than to learn the truth.

Surprisingly, while some people reject what they do not understand, some will accept a statement as true if there is no evidence against it. This is what is often done to the Bible in archeology: "The Bible mentions Hitites, but we have no evidence that there was a Hitite nation, therefore the Bible is in error." This argument is easily defeated when the evidence is eventually found. But until that time, "experts" have a field day with their so called proof. A lack of evidence only means that one cannot conclude whether something is true or false. The lack of evidence is not evidence in and of itself.

A reversal leads to the same false conclusion. Many people are inclined to deny a statement is true if there is a lack of affirming evidence. Consider this flawed argument: "No Moslems are Christians. No Jews are Moslem. Therefore, no Jews are Christian." We may have asserted that Moslems and Christians do not overlap and that Moslems and Jews do not overlap, but we have not proved that Judaism and Christianity are not overlapped conditions. This type of argumentation can be spotted by noting that all the premises and the conclusions are in the negative. However, many people accept this flawed reasoning precisely because there is no positive statement.

One group "proves" that located preachers should not exist by citing situations where located preachers failed to do their duty. I suppose you could list evidence until Judgment Day, but men's failures do not prove whether a duty should or should not exist. If we did accept that line of reasoning, we should say that mankind cannot be saved because they have failed to keep God's law. I'm sure I won't run out of evidence of men's failures, but such evidence doesn't prove man cannot be saved.

The Gravity Game

Have you ever watched a young child toss a toy from their high chair? Mom or dad, distracted by other matters, picks up the toy and the child promptly deposits it over the side again. The game continues ad nauseam until the parent suddenly realizes that they been down this road far too often.

Many holders of false beliefs play the same game. They argue their point and you counter with a well-researched response. Yet, they respond as if you never made a point. While the particular point you address might not be brought up again immediately, it won't be long before you find yourself right back where you started.

I think it is to these types of arguments that Jesus' statement regarding pigs is especially applicable. *"Do not give what is holy to the dogs; nor cast your pearls before swine, lest they trample them under their feet, and turn and tear you in pieces"* (Matthew 7:6). Jewelry is lost on animals. They have no appreciation of its value. Similarly, the truth is lost on some people because they do not have a love for truth (II Thessalonians 2:9-12).

When you find your opponent has no response to your argument, but continually returns to the same invalid point that you disproved, you might consider whether it is worth spending more time debating the point. This is what Paul had to do at times (Acts 13:44-46).

Raising the Bar

When one side successfully answers the points brought up by his opponent, the opponent doesn't admit defeat, instead he demands additional evidence. When I pointed out to a man that James 2:24 proves that a man is not saved by faith alone, his response was that the books of John and Romans never stated that more than faith was necessary for salvation. He was wrong on this point as well, but the tactic was one of raising the bar. He had no answer for the evidence, so he demanded evidence that only came from a particular source.

Another form of this argumentation is to constantly throw out yet another question when previous question is answered. The person hasn't accept the previous answer, but since he doesn't have a response, he will delay a decision until you can answer yet another question. Because there is never any agreement, the questions that must be answered never come to an end.

This tactic has been used to keep men out of the eldership. A congregation studies what is needed for a man to be an elder and several men are offered as meeting those qualifications. If some one doesn't like a particular person or doesn't desire elders, he will find some fault with the man. When the issue is answered, yet another problem will be raised, often by making the terms of qualification stricter than found in the Scriptures or demanding that a particular qualification must be demonstrated in a certain manner. The demand for ever greater and better evidence of qualification continues until the man in question finally gives up and withdraws his name from consideration.

While we desire to answer all questions asked of us (I Peter 3:15), it is well to make sure a point has been addressed before moving on to another. A demand for stronger evidence than required by the Scriptures does not have to be met.

Spurious Precision

This line of argument occurs when a person focus's on minor details instead of the issue at hand, thereby sidetracking the discussion onto irrelevant points. If often happens when a person is unable to grasp the importance of his opponent's logic, so he focuses on a small part and aims his attack at the small piece that he sees. Usually the focus is on a single word, such as President Clinton's infamous response of "It depends on what your meaning of the word "is" is." Such focus on a leaf in the forest keeps the participants from the issues at hand.

Because something is difficult to determine if it is right or wrong, or difficult to define, it is easily ignored. How much hair must one lose to be bald? If I stood several men before you with differing amounts of hair remaining, which ones would you label "bald?" For some, the lack of a precise definition is justification to claim no one is really bald; thereby bypassing the whole uncomfortable position.

This is how the lawyer attempted to handle the uncomfortable conclusion to Jesus' teaching. Faced with proof that he must love his neighbor as himself, he tried to hide behind the imprecise definition of a neighbor (Luke 10:29). Jesus's response proved that he really did not have a difficulty in defining the word neighbor. He understood who among all of mankind was his neighbor (Luke 10:36-37).

Another example of this was when Pilate dismissed Jesus' disturbing statement by asking "What is truth?" (John 18:38).

This same line of argument is used to avoid making a stand on a variety of issues. As an example, since obscenity is hard to crisply define, society has allowed obscenity to proliferate. It is not that people don't understand what is obscene, but they have a problem drawing the line between the obscene and the not so obscene. Rather than make a stand, they avoid the whole issue and accept the unacceptable. A similar issue is defining when life begins. For most it is obvious, but many have accepted definitions that loose or arbitrary. Once a loose definition is accepted, it is easy for people to become more and more tolerant of inappropriate behavior. How short is too short for a dress to be modest? At what point would a man's hair length be considered long? How sound can a church be to be called a sound congregation? We can find a seemingly endless list of issues which people would rather avoid than make a stand.

Every question concerning the meaning of words is not one from spurious precision. Far too often people in denominations attach odd meanings to words, so that two people can say something and both be thinking something different. For example, you could talk with a Roman Catholic about the importance of baptism and appear to be in complete agreement. Yet, you might see baptism as the choice an adult makes to be immersed in water while the Roman Catholic is talking about infant baptism to cleanse the original sin of Adam from the child.

Unproductive Arguments

"Like the legs of the lame that hang limp is a proverb in the mouth of fools. Like one who binds a stone in a sling is he who gives honor to a fool. Like a thorn that goes into the hand of a drunkard is a proverb in the mouth of fools" (Proverbs 26:7-9).

Circular Reasoning

In circular arguments, a person desires to show that certain ideas lead to a conclusion. To prove the point he assumes the conclusion is true and then use it to prove his premise. A classic example is found in the strata and fossil evidence used to argue evolution. A particular strata of rock is declared to be several millions of years old. If you ask how the date was determined you will soon learn that the fossils found within the strata led to date. If you then inquire how they know that the fossils are that old, you are told that it is because they are found in certain rock strata.

Even though circular reasoning is unable to prove its point, those caught up in a circular argument often fail to recognize their problem. They have already accepted both the premise and the conclusion as fact and so it does not bother them if the points are used out of order.

Circular reasoning is not all bad. It can be used to prove equivalence – that is that two ideas stand or fall together, but it does not establish truth. For example, John Calvin's five points are equivalent. He argued that 1) mankind is totally depraved, 2) God unconditionally chooses who will be saved, 3) Christ's death was limited to those so chosen, 4) those so chosen cannot resist God's election, and 5) God will preserve those so chosen. You can start at any one and conclude the others, but none of Calvin's points are true; they are just internally consistent.

Once points are shown to be equivalent, it is possible to uphold or pull down the entire set by dealing with only one point. For example, proving that people are not born totally depraved will cause the collapse of Calvin's entire system.

Unequal Application

Some will agree with a point, but are unable to see that the point requires changes in their own life. It is a common failing in man which led our Savior to state, *"And why do you look at the speck in your brother's eye, but do not consider the plank in your own eye? Or how can you say to your brother, 'Let me remove the speck from your eye'; and look, a plank is in your own eye? Hypocrite! First remove the plank from your own eye, and then you will see clearly to remove the speck from your brother's eye"* (Matthew 7:3-5). We tend to see our own merits but fail to see our own failings, as the Pharisee in Luke 18:9-14. We can see what others need to do, but fail to do it ourselves. Speaking of the Pharisees of his day

Jesus warned, "*Therefore whatever they tell you to observe, that observe and do, but do not do according to their works; for they say, and do not do*" (Matthew 23:3).

Man is not known for his consistency. In discussing the failings of the Jews Paul asked, "*You, therefore, who teach another, do you not teach yourself? You who preach that a man should not steal, do you steal? You who say, "Do not commit adultery," do you commit adultery? You who abhor idols, do you rob temples? You who make your boast in the law, do you dishonor God through breaking the law? For "the name of God is blasphemed among the Gentiles because of you," as it is written*" (Romans 2:21-24). Anytime a religious person is unable to live up to the standard he imposes on others, he degrades the name of God whom he claims to follow. "*They profess to know God, but in works they deny Him, being abominable, disobedient, and disqualified for every good work*" (Titus 1:16).

Knowing this tendency, an effective counter is to present the failing as a problem being dealt with by an unknown third party. Once the person acknowledges that the action is incorrect, you can show him that his own actions are the same. A person of honest heart will then clearly see his own problem. This is how Nathan dealt with David's sin with Bathsheba and the subsequent murder to cover up his sin (II Samuel 12:1-14).

In teaching people about God's plan of salvation, I have noticed a tendency among many to rewrite their personal history to match what they have learned. They are unwilling to think of themselves being in error in the present or in the past. Hence, a baptism when they were infants becomes equivalent to biblical baptism in their minds. To counter this, discuss what a person has done toward their salvation before studying the Scriptures. You might even want write the items down. Then open your Bible and as various topics come up, discuss if they match what was done in the past.

Emotional Arguments

Here the appeal is to a person's heart and not his intellect. Several denominations teach their doctrine in this manner. Mormons will ask you to pray and see if the Holy Spirit doesn't tell you from within that they are right. Pentecostal religions aim for emotional excitement that keeps a person returning for more.

Christianity is not an unemotional religion. There are deep feelings of joy, a solid sense of security, and a firm feeling of duty, responsibility, and purpose in life. All are proper emotions. Even negative emotions have a place in our lives. Christians benefit from feeling a true fear of sin, a deep grief because his fellow man is caught in the bondage of sin, and even a jealousy over the purity of the church and the gospel. Beneficial emotions are the result of our faith, but they are not the source of our faith.

False doctrine is often presented in the midst of emotional preaching, whose purpose is to make people feel good through the use of smooth speech. Unfortunately, smooth speech is popular (II Timothy 4:3-4). It is one of the things that led to the downfall of Israel. *"Who say to the seers, "Do not see," and to the prophets, "Do not prophesy to us right things; speak to us smooth things, prophesy deceits"* (Isaiah 30:10). People much rather be entertained than to hear the truth. But, the position is weak and easily collapses. *"Therefore thus says the Holy One of Israel: "Because you despise this word, and trust in oppression and perversity, and rely on them, therefore this iniquity shall be to you like a breach ready to fall, a bulge in a high wall, whose breaking comes suddenly, in an instant"* (Isaiah 30:12-13).

Sermons should teach the truth and people will react to the message emotionally. Some will be pleased, some grieved, some disgusted and will reject the truth, some will weep and others will rejoice. Notice the reaction Paul received to his sermon on Mars Hill near Athens. *"And when they heard of the resurrection of the dead, some mocked, while others said, "We will hear you again on this matter." So Paul departed from among them. However, some men joined him and believed, among them Dionysius the Areopagite, a woman named Damaris, and others with them"* (Acts 17:32-34).

Appealing to raw emotion is empty. Strong feelings will not make a person a mature Christian. Tear-jerking, heart-pulling speeches will not produce a full-grown child of God. As we read about Jesus, the Master Teacher, in the gospels, we do not see him stooping to such tactics to draw people to him. Dave Miller made this observation in his book *Piloting the Strait*, "Current culture has groomed and conditioned us to be entertained. Television and the cinema have so developed in their sophistication that they are able to stimulate us and hold our attention with little or no effort on our part. As Neil Postman describes in his bestseller *Amusing Ourselves to Death*, we have allowed ourselves to shift away from rational assessment of truth in exchange for substanceless emotional stimulation. So in religious practice, worshipers appear driven by that which is 'better felt than told.'"

Often catch phrases are used to justify indefensible positions, such as "God is too loving to condemn a man eternally in hell." The Scriptures cannot be used to support such a position, so the emotions are appealed to instead.

Emotional appeals are also used to pull the "swing voters." There will always be those uninterested in investing time and effort into learning the details about an issue. So an argument that brings in a strong emotional response will often attract the indecisive. For example, when schools are faced with limited resources and the hard decision comes to cut a portion of the curriculum it will not be the Latin classes which will face the ax. The first programs threaten with extinction are the sports programs because of their popularity. People are willing to pay higher taxes if it means the sports programs can remain. This was the tactic used to get churches to support colleges from their treasury. It was recognized early on that education had little emotional appeal. Instead, the debate focused on churches supporting orphans' homes. Advocates realized that any reasoning that allowed one would allow the other, so the argument that held the greater emotional appeal became the focus. Years after the support of orphans' homes became generally accepted, the support of colleges from the church treasure was re-introduced and this time accepted with little debate.

We need to realize that *"where your treasure is, there your heart will be also"* (Matthew 6:21). What is important to us will drive our emotions. Danger comes when we let our emotions dictate what is important to us.

Examples for Practice

"But solid food belongs to those who are of full age, that is, those who by reason of use have their senses exercised to discern both good and evil" (Hebrews 5:14).

There is no end to the examples which I could present in this chapter. I selected a few dealing with salvation which should illustrate several of the points that I have made. Examine each sample and determine which line of poor reasoning is being used.

The following comes from a discussion I held with a man in the spring of 2002. It represents a unique argument to the question of baptism.

Was water baptism a part of the Law? The answer is "yes"! In the Old Testament it was called "cleansing" -- or "water cleansing". Here is one example of "water cleansing" in the Old Testament, of which Israel was under the Law, of those things that were not clean. Leviticus 11:32, "it "must" be put into water, and it shall be unclean until the even; so it shall be cleansed (read the context , by reading verses 22 thru verse 47).

Jesus Christ fulfilled the law, and thus was "water baptized" - "water cleansed". Jesus Christ said this is my body which is given for you - "take eat", and this is my blood of the new and everlasting covenant, take and drink. Before Jesus Christ could offer himself, he needed to fulfill the law of "water cleansing" - "water baptism". John "cleansed" - "baptized" with water, which fulfilled the law. This is the "reason" that Jesus Christ was baptized with water. Another record of water cleansing is in Leviticus 15:13. Jesus Christ had no need to be water cleansed, as he was sinless. But he came also to "fulfill" the law of Moses, also called the Law of God.

So, is there a "need" to be "water baptized" anymore ? NO ! The Law has been fulfilled, and there is no need to continue to "do" the law. If we were to continue to "do" the law, then Christ has been made of no affect unto you , and you

then who have been saved , fall from grace -
Galatians chapter 5.

The following came from a mass mailing sent to preachers across the United States in December of 2003.

For many years the churches of Christ have used Matthew 28:19 as a baptism that adds to the church that was built by the word of the Lord that went forth from Jerusalem, a baptism that was not present when Israel was told to repent and be baptized in the name of Jesus Christ. Search the scriptures and you will not find this commandment in Jerusalem as the Lord's church was being opened to the inhabitants of Jerusalem. If you look at the dates of these writings you will find that Matthew was not inspired by the Spirit to write the book we know as Matthew until the church had been established for about seven years. If the church of Christ that came by the preaching of the gospel of Christ on the day of Pentecost was built complete seven years before Matthew by the Spirit of God revealed it in the book that carries his name, why are men destined to bring Matthew 28:19 into the church today which is as unlawful as no baptism at all into the lives of the people which cannot forgive sin?

Where is the power of God that will save the people from their sins? Study the promise that Jesus made to the disciples at John 14:26 & John 16:13, this is where you will find the power of God that will save the world from sin. What God translated by His Spirit has harmonized every word that Jesus said to the disciples as long as He was in the world. There is no baptism in the name of the Father, Son and Holy Ghost for the remission of sins that will add

---

anyone to His church. It was not present on the day of Pentecost for the church, it is not present for the church today. Let God lead you into His kingdom, and give up this doctrine that has no strength to save anyone. All scripture is given by the inspiration which is profitable for correction.

I did respond with a letter giving details of why this man's teachings were false. His response to my letter is also instructive.

From what I have just read in your response, you might just as well have discarded it. You understood nothing about what was written in the Letter of Concern. When you are born into the kingdom of God, that birth must be in the name of Jesus Christ, through the head of the church. Matthew contributed nothing to the establishment of the church on the day of Pentecost. If you do have some understanding of the inspired scriptures, you will see that Peter was the only apostle to receive the keys of the kingdom of heaven, Mt.16:19. Matthew was not included in this promise as Peter was, therefore, the church came into the world through the exact words that came from the mouth of Peter, and that my friend is the sum total of what Jesus revealed by the Spirit of God on that great day. Every time Matthew 28:19 is brought into baptism in the Lord's church, what Jesus promised in the gospel of John has been made void, and nothing and nobody is saved.

Yes, I am an ignorant man when it comes to the perfection of God, but by reading some of these e-mails, I can truthfully say, some men are only a step behind me. Men build themselves up in their own eyes, and in their own ability to teach others, and these men are not teachers at all, and will probably remain babes as long as they live.

I am truly sorry that this discussion has gone this way, I was honest in what I wrote to the churches of Christ, but some men are not yet prepared to receive the simplicity that Jesus has offered to them. I am not to hurt or offend any man, and Jesus says; It is impossible that offenses come, but woe to that man through whom they come. Think before you write, and what you have written has not offended me at all, but what you have written may have offended the Lord. Be careful.

The following is taken from a discussion of whether baptism is necessary for salvation. This response illustrates several ways to refute the obvious.

In Acts 22 Paul said, "*Arise and be baptized. and wash away your sins, calling on the name of the Lord*" (Acts 22:16). Does this verse not say that being baptized washes away ones sins?

No! In the first place, the word "and" between "arise" and "be baptized" is not in the Greek text. In the next place, in the Greek text this sentence consists of two clauses each consisting of a command and a participle:

1. Arising, be baptized
2. Be washed, having called

The two verbs *(arising* and *having called)* are aorist participles meaning that the action of the participle comes before the action of the command. In other words, when we take into consideration the construction of the Greek text and the meaning of the participles, an accurate interpretation would be that *arising* comes before baptism and *calling* comes before washing. A proper translation, then, would be "now that you have called on the Lord and had your sins washed away, arise and be baptized." The chronological order of the various elements is as follows: calling, washing, arising, and baptizing. This verse does not teach that baptism is necessary for the forgiveness of sins.

The same author wrote the following concerning Acts 2:38.

Take two aspirins for a headache. Does that mean that you take two aspirins and you will have a headache? No! You take two aspirins BECAUSE OF a headache. Likewise one is baptized because his sins have been remitted. Baptism is for Christians, not people who are still in their sins.

While strongly written, the following does show the attitudes of many to the truth.

With imbeciles it's easier to "rear back" as you put it... "Believe on the Lord Jesus Christ and thou shalt be saved". Repentance is a given. Want to see if you can complicate it a little more? Remember when Christ roamed the earth preaching, he preached to a very uneducated people. That's why there are so many parables in the Bible, that's the only way he could make them understand. You idiots that think you have to take the Bible absolutely literally, are delusional and will remain that way until you wake up. This is not complicated folks, all you have to do is believe and accept, it's that simple, it really is. And to add a little more fuel to the fire, once you are saved, you belong to God, you are always saved, you cannot lose your salvation - PERIOD. So all you "educated" fruitcakes that think you know the Bible can come out of the woodwork now and "prove" me wrong. I could use a good laugh right now.

---

www.ingramcontent.com/pod-product-compliance
Lightning Source LLC
Chambersburg PA
CBHW032000040426
42448CB00006B/434